What Every Girl Should Know

A Mother-Daughter Bible Study Designed for Girls

Victoria L. Barnes

First Printing 1997
Second Printing 2001

What Every Girl Should Know
A Mother-Daughter Bible Study Designed for Girls

Executive Editor: Anne Burnson

Published by Calvary Missionary Press, PO Box 13532 Tucson, Arizona 85732.

Printed in the United States of America

Library of Congress Cataloging in Publication Data

Barnes, Victoria.
What Every Girl Should Know
A Mother-Daughter Bible Study Designed for Girls

Library of Congress Catalog Number

ISBN   0-912375-05-1

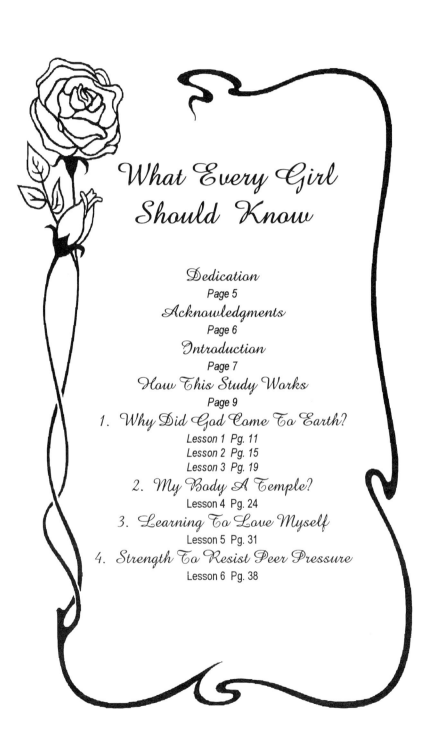

What Every Girl Should Know

Dedication

Never in my wildest dreams did I ever envision that a daughter could bless my life as much as my daughter Kristin has. The Lord has truly been good to me beyond measure with His wonderful gift of her life. The privilege of watching her grow and observing her love for the Lord as well as her desire to please Him, is a joy worth more to me than the richest of treasures. Therefore, it is with my deepest love that I dedicate this work to the Lord and to Kristin. I love you.

Acknowledgments

I've always been the type of person who has noticed when things needed to be done, and I have always jumped right in and gotten them done. I have seldom been afraid to tackle a project I believed in. However, when I felt God's conviction to write this study, I knew I was not equipped to take on the project. Through the numerous hours, weeks, and months of relying on the Lord for direction, I realized once again that when God calls us to take a step of faith, He is not only right there, but He also provides people to come alongside to uphold, encourage, and strengthen us that we might complete the work He has called us to do.

I would like to recognize some of the people who contributed to making this Bible study a reality. Although some may feel that their part was a small one, often their words were like "*apples of gold in settings of silver* " (Proverbs 25:11).

First, I would like to thank my husband Joe for the endless encouragement he faithfully and consistently gave me. He continually motivated me to persevere and assisted me in learning the necessary computer skills required for putting the study together.

Pastor Ralph Porter faithfully reviewed each lesson and kept his doors open whenever I needed help. His loyalty and encouragement gave me the confidence I needed.

I would also like to thank Dr. Richard Ruiz and Dr. Tom Tompkins for their dedication in reviewing the study and for providing helpful advice. Their affirmation of the study was a wonderful blessing.

The medical content of this study would not have been possible without Dr. Mary Beth Adam's expertise in the area of adolescent gynecology and development, as well as her motivation and encouragement.

Finally, I want to thank Anne Burnson and Scott Coverdale for the many hours of faithful dedication in editing and clarification.

Without the assistance of these and many other steadfast friends in our church family, *What Every Girl Should Know* would not be a reality today.

Thank you for your support.

Introduction

My desire to help teenage girls initially began when I volunteered as a counselor for the Crisis Pregnancy Centers. Through the course of time I became increasingly interested in the pressures and problems faced by teenage girls. I have to admit that when I first began to volunteer, my main goal was to convince these young women not to terminate their unwanted pregnancies. My heart ached to think that such a precious gift as a baby could be literally thrown away. Through the years, however, as I listened to the heartbreaking stories these young women told about their lives and what led them to such a frightening and lonely predicament, my focus shifted from the "endangered" pregnancy to the "endangered" teenager. These girls had many distorted notions and confused ideas about not only their sexuality, but also their value as young women. Their beliefs about self and sexuality were derived from media images, peers, and the misinformed guidance of significant people in their lives.

To me, the tragedy was not just the wasted lives of these babies, but also the misdirected lives of these girls. If a difference were to be made, these girls would need to have God's principles revealed to them in a way that would enable them to make informed choices that would have a positive impact on their future.

With this study it is my desire to provide girls with the solid foundation of biblical truths that our society is trying so desperately to eliminate. Hopefully, if preteen and teenage girls are presented with an accurate picture of what it means to be a healthy, self-assured woman, loved by God, they will be successful in resisting the pressures and misconceptions that teens so often face.

Through God's Word, girls will be equipped with facts that will enable them to make good choices throughout their lives and become godly women. We are daughters of the King! We are called to live lives that will bring honor and glory to our Father in heaven.

As you work together through *What Every Girl Should Know*, may you gain deeper insights into the love God has for each of you and grow in your relationship as mother and daughter or as an older woman encouraging a younger woman.

" Therefore… let us throw off everything that hinders and the sin that so easily entangles, and let us run with perseverance the race marked out for us."

Hebrews 12:1

How This Study Works

The goal of *What Every Girl Should Know* is to develop spiritual growth in each study group member and to encourage each girl to make a personal commitment to God based on her *own* knowledge of what God's Word says. When children are born into a Christian home they may accept Jesus at a young age and believe what is taught to them by their parents or by their church. This Bible study course will help each girl decide *for herself*, perhaps for the first time, what *she* believes based on *her own* in-depth study of what Scripture says. This study is designed to strengthen each member in the principles of a God-centered life. It is also meant to build relationships between mothers and daughters or perhaps between an older woman and a special girl, and open up lines of communication in otherwise difficult topics. Finally, this study will provide an opportunity for each girl to privately make a promise before the Lord and her parents to maintain her sexual purity and honor God with her body.

Considering the busy school schedules of girls in this age group who are preoccupied with homework, sports, music, and church activities, some may be hesitant to add another commitment to an already full life. Taking this into account, the *What Every Girl Should Know* Bible study course has been designed to make it easy for everyone to participate. Even those with the most hectic schedules will find that taking part in this Bible study course is possible without creating unnecessary pressure. For this reason, this study is intended to be worked through together as a small group. Mother and daughter teams will meet together once a week to study God's Word and discuss the topic of the week. However, if everyone's schedule allows and the group prefers it, you may choose to work on lessons in advance as mother-daughter teams, then come together each week to review and discuss the topics. Either way, you will enjoy learning together what God's desire is for your lives.

Each topic will build on the next, so it is important that you make a commitment to attend each session. If it is necessary for you to miss a lesson, you should complete the missed lesson together (mother-daughter team) before you meet with your group. This study is designed to be used in a small group setting which can include between six and eight mother-daughter teams, or twelve to sixteen people.

After the initial orientation meeting, there are fifteen lessons in this study. Each lesson should take approximately one and a half hours, depending on how the schedule is set up. This allows time for a short break, yet gets everyone home early. It is recommended that the time of at least one session be lengthened to provide an opportunity to meet as a group for dinner, or perhaps dessert or ice cream. This social gathering will enable group members to strengthen relationships with one another and form lasting friendships. A sample of a typical lesson schedule is as follows:

      10 min. Welcome and opening prayer.
      30 min. Study God's Word and lesson topic.
      10 min. Break/snack.
      30 min. Continue lesson and discussion.
      10 min. Take prayer requests and close in prayer.

Note: On the day or days that are designated for dinner or dessert, the meeting should begin at least one hour earlier or the lesson time should be extended.

Each group member is instructed to complete every lesson thoroughly in her own workbook and discuss it further as individual mother-daughter teams after the group session. This discussion will encourage further communication about the topic and help strengthen your relationship.

Upon completing the *What Every Girl Should Know* Bible study course, the group leader will review the study books to verify completion. Each girl who completes the entire course will graduate and receive a diploma.

In today's society, maturing in godliness can sometimes be difficult and confusing since so many mixed messages are being received from various sources. *What Every Girl Should Know* Bible, in conjunction with God's Word, will equip you to evaluate the messages our society sends, and identify their validity based on what Scripture says. Through His Word, God will help you understand that there is hope even in hopeless and confusing situations, and direct your path in the way of righteousness.

May you experience God's richest blessings as you seek to live your life for Him.

Why Did God Come to Earth?

LESSON 1

In this chapter, we will focus on God's desire to have *fellowship* with us. In the first three lessons, we will study how God, from the beginning of Creation, devised ways to be close to us and how He patiently guides His people to His ultimate demonstration of love.

The Bible tells us that God created the universe. Some of us have read and heard the Creation story many times, in different forms, from many people. The purpose of this lesson is to assist you in investigating for yourself, with other girls your age, why you believe this "truth" that your parents or the church have taught you. Perhaps for the first time, you will be able to acknowledge it as the only *real* Truth, on your own. If you have never really heard the Creation story at all, or maybe you've heard it only in parts, this lesson will unravel for you the foundational principles of what God's desire for man is and why He ultimately came to earth.

Whether you are new to studying the Bible or have lots of experience, you will enjoy the freedom of exploring these facts with other mother-daughter teams in your group. Whenever Bible verses are mentioned in our study, please turn to each verse so that together, we can see firsthand what God's true desire is for our lives.

Note: The New International Version (NIV) of the Bible is used throughout this study. Although other translations are acceptable, we suggest you use an NIV Bible when available.

Read Genesis 1-3 aloud together.

Inspired by the Holy Spirit, Moses, the author of the book of Genesis, relates to us that God is the creator of all life.

1. Read Genesis 1:26 and 3:22. Was God alone? What does this tell you about the Trinity (God the Father, Son, and the Holy Spirit)?

2. Read John 1:1-2. Who was with God in the beginning?

3. What does John 1:14 say about who "the Word" is?

4. Read Gen. 3:8-11 again. What was God doing in the garden? What can you see in these verses about God and His relationship with Adam?

God, the Creator of all life, made us in *His image* (Gen. 1:27) giving us life, personality, truth, wisdom, love, holiness, justice and individuality. However, when Eve gave in to the serpent's lie and was deceived, sin entered the world in the form of the knowledge of good and evil (Gen. 3:22). The holiness that had been breathed into man (Gen. 2:7) was now ruined by Adam and Eve's disobedience which began with Eve's choice to satisfy her own desires. **Discuss Genesis 2:7.**

5. In your own words, tell what the "knowledge of good and evil" means. Please give an example.

6. Why does sin separate us from God (Hab. 1:13a)?

7. How can some of the choices we make affect others?

8. How can we be sure that we are making good choices?

9. What happened to Adam's relationship with God after he chose to sin by disobeying God's command (Gen. 3:23)?

10. Write down any questions you may have concerning this lesson.

         God is a caring God. The fact that He clothed Adam and Eve (Gen. 3:21) after they sinned testifies to His compassion. An animal was sacrificed to provide garments of skin, and later, all Israel's animal sacrifices would be part of God's provision to remedy the curse of sin and separation from God—a life for a life (Hebrews 9:22).

11. How can knowing this truth about how God loves us help you in your relationship with Him?

"I will walk among you and be your God, and you will be my people."

Leviticus 26:12

14

Why Did God Come to Earth?

LESSON 2

In Lesson 1, we learned that God and man were separated because of man's sin. Although the Lord did not dwell with man again after the fall of Adam and Eve, we know that God did not abandon man. He spoke to Cain and Abel (Gen. 4), He instructed Noah on the building of the ark (Gen. 6), He made a covenant with Abraham (Gen. 15), and He used Moses to set His people free from slavery to the Egyptians (Ex. 12: 31-42).

God's desire to have fellowship with man continued. The Israelites had suffered a great deal under the oppression of their Egyptian masters, who *"made their lives bitter with hard labor"* (Ex. 1:14). They had been slaves to the Egyptians for four hundred years, yet God set them free. While traveling out of Egypt through the desert, their faith had been tested. Prior to the parting of the Red Sea (Ex. 14), God provided quail and manna when they were starving (Ex. 16), and water from the rock when they were thirsty (Ex. 17). Now, Moses is up on Mount Sinai, the mountain of God (Ex. 24:13), and God is giving Moses instructions for building the tabernacle.

Throughout these many trials, we continue to see God's faithfulness despite His people's continued sin.

Read Exodus 24:1- 25:9 aloud together.

1. What kind of offerings did God tell Moses he wanted from the people (Ex. 25:2)?

2. What does this tell you about the kind of relationship God desires from us?

3. What does God promise in Ex. 25:8 once the sanctuary is built?

Read Exodus 32:1-14

4. According to Ex. 32:1-14, what did the Israelites choose to do when they thought that Moses was not coming back (v. 8)?

5. The Israelites had received the Ten Commandments from God (Ex. 20), yet willfully decided to break the second commandment. Although God's anger burned against the Israelites (Ex. 32:10), He did not bring disaster upon His people (Ex. 32:14). What does this show us about God's character?

6. All sin has consequences. Not all the people, however, had given in to idolatry (Ex. 32:26). The people who continued in their sin were killed (v. 27). Those who were not killed but continued to

sin died from a plague (v. 35). What does Rom. 6:23 tell us about sin?

7. Based upon Exodus 32, what truths can we learn about obedience? What role does peer pressure play in this incident (vv. 21,26,29)?

Read Exodus 40:34-38 aloud together.

8. Was this the type of fellowship God had with Adam? Why? Why not?

9. Why do you think God could not have the same fellowship with the Israelites that He had with Adam before the Fall (Isa. 59:2)?

10. When we sin, we are separated from God (Isa. 59:2). Does the principle that sin "separates" also hold true for our relationships with one another here on earth? Give an example.

From the time that God's glory filled the tabernacle (Ex. 40:34), God remained with the Israelites through all their travels (v. 38). Now we will look at how God desires to establish an earthly dwelling in the form of a temple. This man-made temple will later be replaced by the living temple of each believer's body.

Read II Samuel 7:1-16

11. What message does God give the prophet Nathan to give to King David about building a dwelling for God (v. 13)?

12. What encouragement can you find in knowing the truth concerning God's character?

13. What are some lessons you can learn from the Israelites' mistakes that can help you to be faithful to God?

"Your love, O LORD, reaches to the heavens,
your faithfulness to the skies."
Psalm 36:5

18

Why Did God Come to Earth?

LESSON 3

In Lesson 2, we learned that although God no longer dwells with man as He had in the garden, He does not abandon His people, but continues to reach out to them in spite of their sin. Once again we see God's love and faithfulness displayed in action when He fulfills the promise He made to King David through the prophet Nathan.

Four hundred and eighty years after the Exodus, David's son, King Solomon, begins work on the greatest project of his life: the building of the temple for the Lord's dwelling. It takes Solomon seven years to complete the temple. Once the temple is complete, Solomon dedicates it to the Lord (I Kings 8:22-53).

Read I Kings 6:1 & 11-16

1. What does the Lord tell Solomon He will do when the temple is built (I Kings 6:13)?

2. What must Solomon do for this to happen (v. 12) ? Can someone really do this (James 2:10)?

19

Read 1 Kings 8:6-14

3. According to verse 11, does the Lord fulfill the promise He gave to King David in II Sam. 7:13 and to King Solomon in I Kings 6:13?

4. God continues to reveal His desire to have fellowship with man. What does this teach us about God and His promises (I Kings 8:24)?

5. Write Numbers 23:19 in your own words.

Read Ezekiel 8:4-10

6. The glory of God filled the temple just as He had promised. In Ezekiel's vision, what had the people of Israel done?

Read Ezekiel 10: 4 & 18, and 11:23

7. What was the consequence of their disobedience? Briefly

discuss what was happening in these verses and why it was happening.

We now come to the greatest demonstration of love in the history of mankind. At the perfect time, God sends His Son to live and walk with us here on earth. Jesus willingly becomes the last sin offering that ever has to be made. You may remember from Lesson 1 that after Adam and Eve sinned, God made garments for them from animal skins. This event was the first sin offering. Now, Jesus Christ gives himself up as the last sacrifice. One man's sin (Adam's) becomes eternal death to many, and another Man's death (Christ's) becomes eternal life for many (Rom. 5:12, 15). No other sacrifice will ever have to be made (Heb. 10:12, 17-18). Christ took all our sins to the grave, only to replace them with His righteousness which is *given* to us when *we* choose to put *our faith* in Him (Rom. 3:22 and 5:19).

Read John 1:1-14

8. According to this passage, who lived with us for a while (v. 14)?

9. Over and over, God's chosen people sin against Him. Over and over, God faithfully provides a way for them to repent and turn to Him. Why do you suppose God didn't give up and destroy men as he did in the golden calf incident (Ex. 32:10)?

Read I John 4:7-19

21

As we stated in the first lesson, many of you have grown up going to church and hearing your parents tell you about their faith in Jesus Christ. As a result, some of you may have received Jesus as very young children and you may have been baptized. Up until this time, you may have been comfortable believing what your parents and your church have told you. Now, however, based on the truths *you* have learned about God and what He wants from us, you may want to recommit your life to Him based upon your *own* belief. God gives us the ability to choose whether we will put our faith in Him or not. Scripture tells us that no man comes to the Father except through Christ (John 14:6).

10. Why did God come to earth?

11. Are you willing to commit your life to God based on the truth *you* now know?

12. Look up John 1:12. What does it mean? Please write the verse in your own words.

13. All who receive Christ and believe in Him become children of God. If you have chosen to place your trust in Jesus or have

recommitted you life to Him based on these truths you have learned, write your name and the date here.

"For the LORD is good and his love endures forever;
his faithfulness continues through all generations."
Psalm 100:5

My Body A Temple?

LESSON 4

In the first three lessons of our study, we followed God through the Scriptures, and discovered together His desire to have fellowship with us. We learned how God's love and faithfulness never failed despite the continued sinfulness of His people. Finally, we saw His greatest demonstration of love when He sent His own Son to be the ultimate sacrifice that would unite what sin had separated: A holy God from His people.

By Christ's blood, we are no longer held guilty of our sin, and therefore, are no longer separated from God. Do we still sin? Yes! Should we be held guilty of our sins and pay the penalty? Yes! But, because of God's great love, we are not condemned for our sins as long as **we choose** to accept Christ as **our** Savior. Christ paid the price so that our sins will not be counted against us. As a result, we are washed clean and our sins are replaced by Christ's righteousness. We are now free to have fellowship with God (Rom. 3:25-26). Of course, we have a choice. God will not force us to love and serve Him. The choice is ours. We cannot rely on our parents' faith, or on what our church has taught us for our personal salvation. We learned that *we* must say, **"I choose Christ, because I believe in Him."**

Once we have made the decision to accept Christ as our personal Savior, Christ becomes the mediator between us and God. God looks down at us and sees us through Jesus. Let me give you an example. When the sun is very bright, the light hurts our eyes. As a matter of fact, we cannot look directly at the sun for an extended period of time without permanently damaging our eyes. So, we put on some dark sunglasses and our eyes feel better instantly. Likewise, our sins grieve God deeply. He is too holy to look at our sin. So, He sees us through Jesus' righteousness (kind of God's Son-glasses). God no longer sees our sins; instead He sees the purity of Christ's righteousness which is more beautiful than freshly fallen snow. Therefore, there is nothing to separate us from the love of God. The Bible tells us that if we choose Christ as our Savior and are repentant of our sins, God chooses not to remember our sins and no longer holds them against us (Heb. 10:17).

As Christians, because of Christ's death on the cross, we are now clean from sin. At the time we accepted Christ (God the Son), whether it was a long time ago or just recently, God the Father sends the Holy Spirit (God the Holy Spirit) to live inside us (Gal. 4:4-6).

In our past lessons, we saw the various ways in which God dwelt among men. He dwelt visibly with Adam and Eve in the garden. Later, His glory filled the tabernacle in Moses' time and the temple in Solomon's time. Finally, God sent His Son to live among us for a while. During the time Christ was on earth, He was physically present among us in the form of a man.

Today, God dwells in every believer in the form of the Holy Spirit. "Where's the temple?" you might ask. Remember we talked about Jesus Christ being your personal Savior? Well, if you have chosen to accept Christ, God lives in you in the person of the Holy Spirit (Rom. 8:9-11).

In this chapter, we will learn together how our bodies serve as a temple for the Holy Spirit of God. We will look at examples of what God desires from us as we live to serve and enjoy Him.

When God sent His Son to earth to dwell among us, He had a mission in mind. Christ was to show us the way to the Father (John 14:6). Scripture states clearly that we all like sheep have gone astray, and each of us has turned to our own way (Isa. 53:6). We hadn't been able to figure it out on our own; and even if we had, there was nothing we could accomplish by relying on ourselves to earn salvation (Eph. 2:8-9).

When Christ's time on earth was nearing an end, He comforted His disciples by promising that when He left, God would not leave them alone. He would send a Counselor (the Holy Spirit) to live in them.

Read John 14

1. What does Jesus say we will do if we love Him (vv. 15, 23)?

2. Does Jesus ask us to do something He Himself is not prepared to do (v. 31)?

3. How far did Jesus take His obedience?

4. How long does Jesus tell His disciples the Holy Spirit will be with them (v.16)?

5. What does "*We will come to him and make our home with him*" mean to you (v.14:23b)?

6. God has not left us alone. He will send the Holy Spirit in Jesus' place to do what two things (v. 26)?

Read John 16: 1-16

7. According to verse 13, what will one of the Holy Spirit's jobs be?

8. Tell what verse 13 means in your own words.

Read I Cor. 6: 12-20

Because God does not hold us hostage and force us to do His will, we are at liberty to do what we choose (I Cor. 6:12a).

9.   What do you think Paul (the author of this book) meant by the words "*Everything is permissible for me, but not everything is beneficial*" and "*I will not be mastered by anything*?"

10a. Give an example of something that may be permissible for you, yet not beneficial.

b. What does it mean to be "mastered" by something?

11. Our bodies are a member of whom according to verse 15?

12. What does "*you are not your own; you were bought at a price*" mean (vv. 19b-20a)?

13a. What does Scripture say God wants us to do with our bodies (v. 20b)?

b. Give two or three examples of how we can honor God with our bodies.

14. Do you think drug and alcohol abuse keeps us from honoring God? Explain. What does too much wine do to God's temple (Prov. 20:1, Isa. 5:22, Eph. 5:18)?

15. What are some other things that can corrupt God's temple?

16. How should knowing this truth affect the choices we make?

17. What is one positive thing you can begin to do today to keep God's temple holy?

As believers we are one with Christ. Everything we do with our bodies (His temple) will involve Christ. It doesn't matter how insignificant we may think it is; our choices affect the Lord.

Christ is not the only one who is affected when we sin with our bodies. In verse 19 we see that our choices also involve the Holy Spirit. Since it is God who sends the Holy Spirit to dwell in us, He too is grieved.

The Holy Spirit dwells in each of us as believers. Together as the church, we make up the body of Christ. As members of this body, we must try to work together to peacefully keep the body of Christ united. Our bodies are members of the larger body of Christ: the Church.

So, what does this all mean to us? Considering all that God has done for us since the beginning of mankind, wouldn't it be appropriate for us to give ourselves back to God? After all, "...*God demonstrates his own love for us in this: While we were still sinners, Christ died for us*" (Rom. 5:8).

"Do you not know that your body is a temple of the Holy Spirit, who is in you, whom you have received from God? You are not your own; you were bought at a price. Therefore honor God with your body."
I Corinthians 6.19

30

Learning to Love Myself

LESSON 5

We are made in God's image. God has breathed life into us. All through the Scriptures, we see the importance and value God places on each one of us as His children. God did not just randomly throw us together when He created us. Consider how intricately and perfectly our body parts function together.   In spite of technological advances and vast developments in medical science, there is no human being in the history of the world who can say that he has made another human being from scratch. Our bodies are just one evidence of God's omnipotence. God loves us and wants us to understand how valuable we are to Him. However, it is important that we learn to see ourselves in a way that is honoring to God. If we do not value ourselves properly, it makes it difficult for us to love others the way God wants us to. On the other hand, if we exaggerate our own importance, we are too full of ourselves to be bothered with loving others. God commands us to love others as much as we love ourselves. A balance is crucial. Together we will take a look at various passages of Scripture that will help us understand what a healthy view of self is.

The world around us constantly tells us that we should "look out for number one" and "if it feels good, do it." God certainly wants us to take care of ourselves and feel good, but not at the expense of others. Television programming is saturated with beautiful men and women who give us the feeling that if we are not attractive, we are not worth much. The media bombards us with messages that male-female relationships should start very early and have little or no restrictions. Sin looks so good that we as Christians often feel as if we are missing out. Unfortunately, what television doesn't show us are the consequences that occur as a result of these apparently carefree lifestyles. Psalm 73 helps us understand that we are not alone in feeling left out of the "fun," and what happens to people who choose to live in sin.

Read Psalm 73: discuss briefly.

The writer of this psalm almost slipped when he saw the "fun" the ungodly were having. His envy overwhelmed him until he entered the sanctuary of God. Then he could understand the benefits of his faith in God.

During adolescence, our bodies undergo such big changes that often we don't understand what's going on, even when it's been explained to us. Somehow, living through the preteen and teenage years is a whole different story than hearing or even reading about it. This time in our lives can sometimes be very painful.

It is not uncommon for us to feel badly about the way we look, act, and sound, or about how tall, short, slender or heavy we are. At this age, we are very aware of our bodies and our friends' bodies, and often we compare ourselves to others and feel envious. If we are developing quickly, we sometimes feel out of place because our bodies look more like the bodies of adults. If we are not developing at the same speed as our friends, we feel horrible because we look like kids and immediately think that there must be something wrong with us. Please understand that during these years, you are "under construction." Each one of us is uniquely different. If you look at all the moms in the room, you will see that even after the "construction" is over, we are all different. The most important thing to remember is that God loves each one of us and wants us to understand how valuable we are to Him. After all, He made us just the way we are and has a special plan for each one of us.

Thank God that we are unique. Can you imagine what a boring place the world would be if we all had brown hair, brown eyes, and the same height, weight and body form? That might be fun for ten minutes, but after a while, we would get sick of looking at ourselves everywhere we went. It sure is great to know how special we are to God!

In this lesson, we will see that God knows each one of us personally, intimately, and individually. This lesson will also help us to see the special place God has given us here on earth and the importance of maintaining a proper view of ourselves. This balance will enable us to love and value others, and by doing so, bring honor and glory to God.

Read Psalm 139

1. In verse 13 we read that God created our innermost being. During what stage of our life does this verse say God is present?

2. How does verse 14 describe the way we are made?

3. What does verse 14 say about God's works?

4. If we believe that God's works are wonderful and Scripture tells us that we are wonderfully made, why do you think it is important for us to see ourselves the way God sees us?

5. Discuss the meaning of verse 16b with the group. Tell what this verse means in your own words.

Read Psalm 8

King David, (the author of this psalm) describes God's majesty as seen throughout His creation over all the earth. God's glory is exalted high above the heavens (verse 1). Then David considers God's work in creation. Recognizing how awesome God's power is, David realizes how insignificant man is by comparison.

6. What does verse 4 say about how God feels about us?

7. What position does verse 5 say God has given us, and what has He put us in charge of (vv. 6-8)?

Note: The King James and American Standard versions translate "heavenly beings" as angels.

8. Knowing the position God has given us and how He feels about us, how should we feel about ourselves?

9. Briefly write a short list of the gifts, position and status we have in God's sight as believers.

Knowing what a special place we hold as God's children is enough to make us think and feel as if we *are* number one. Furthermore, the position we occupy is so important that each one of us should have our own personal maidservant. Right? (I'm not talking about your mom, either.) Let's see what Scripture has to say about that.

Read Philippians 2:1-11

In Christ we have encouragement (from the Counselor, the Holy Spirit), comfort from knowing how much God loves us, fellowship with the Holy Spirit who lives in us, and tenderness and compassion toward other believers.

10. Because we are given so much, what does Scripture tell us we should and should not do (vv. 3-4)?

11. Why should we, as daughters of the King, not be selfish, vain, or conceited, but consider others as better than ourselves to the point of putting them first (vv. 5-8)?

Read Mark 10:42-45

12. For what reasons did Christ come to earth (v. 45)?

13. What do verses 43 and 44 say about who will be great in heaven?

We are very special to God. However, we are called to serve, not to be served. Only Christ *is* number one. He alone had every right to have personal servants, yet He willingly gave up that right and became a servant to all.

Read I Peter 3:3-4

14. Where should our beauty come from (vv.3-4)?

15. Discuss what a gentle and quiet spirit means (v. 4).

16. What do the clothes we wear say about us?

17. What does verse 3 tell us about the wrong reason for choosing what to wear?

18. Knowing how God feels about us, how should this truth affect the way we feel about ourselves? About God?

It is truly a privilege to be considered a daughter of God. When we aren't sure how we feel about ourselves, when our bodies aren't exactly the way we would like them to be, even when we don't like ourselves very much, we can be confident beyond a shadow of a doubt that God's love is steadfast. He will never leave us nor forsake us (Heb. 13:5b). Our parents will show us love in many ways, but their love is only a small reflection of the unsurpassed, unconditional love that God has for each individual. He is intimately aware of every last one of us even before we are born, while we are still in the womb, and then throughout our entire lives. In His love, He freely gives each of us the choice to spend eternity in heaven with him as His very special princess.

"For I know the plans I have for you," declares the LORD, "plans to prosper you and not to harm you, plans to give you hope and a future."

Jeremiah 29:11

Strength To Resist Peer Pressure

LESSON 6

Life is like a 3-D jigsaw puzzle. Our individual "life puzzles" are neatly planned in advance by God who knows how each piece will ultimately fall into place. We begin with very little awareness of God's plan. When we are toddlers, we cannot seem to understand what is going on around us, so we just stare at the mess of puzzle pieces around us. As we get a little older, we learn that there is a certain order that must be followed if pieces are going to fit together the right way. For example, we coo before we talk, crawl before we walk, obey to avoid time-outs, and are trusted by others as a result of our honesty. Slowly, as we put the pieces of our "life puzzle" together, we gain experience and knowledge from life situations, and if we accept God's "instruction book," the Bible, we can be certain that each piece will fall into place according to God's plan. There are times when our "life puzzle" gets really tough to put together because the pieces of our life seem confusing and unclear. If we continue to follow God's instructions on putting the puzzle together, the problems, although still there, are bearable and we can have peace in knowing that we are on the right track. Sometimes our problems seem as if they are never going to end, but if we have faith that God desires the very best for us, then later we may begin to see the beautiful picture of God's plan emerging.

Although difficult and confusing times can occur at almost any point in our lives, they quite frequently happen during adolescence. So much change is going on with our bodies and with what is expected of us that we forget to rely on the "instruction book" that came with our "life puzzle." After all, this "instruction book" has all the principles we need to live by and will never lead us astray.

We've learned how valuable we are to God, and how important a proper balance is in valuing ourselves and others. One big concern we may have at this stage in our "life puzzle" is the need for our friends to like us. All of us need to be loved and accepted. Often, we measure how "valuable" we are by how our friends see us. We want to look, act, talk and dress like our peers. One problem with this is that we forget that our friends are *also* going through the same confusing stage we are, and they may not be thinking clearly either. Peer pressure can be so strong that it can lead us to do things that we believe are wrong and sinful in God's sight.

Peer pressure or conformity does not only affect adolescents. Adults also struggle with the pressure to give in to what their peers are doing in order to avoid rejection, ridicule, or just to fit in. Here's an example: Our family has gone to church for many years. When my husband and I first accepted the Lord, most of our friends were not Christians. Whenever we got together with our church friends, it was easy to bow our heads and ask God to bless our meal. However, when we were with our old, non-church friends, it was very hard to bow our heads and thank God for our food. We were afraid that our friends would see us and call us fanatics. We knew this was wrong and asked God to help us be bold and not ashamed. Soon, not only did we bow our heads to give thanks for our food, but we asked our friends to join us in doing so. Scripture tells us that the only thing we are to conform to is the likeness of Christ. Thank God, we can rely on Him to supply the strength and boldness we need to stand up under pressure.

Putting together the pieces of our "life puzzle" takes an entire lifetime. As we get older, each life stage or situation becomes a new or different piece for us to handle and make sense of. Some fit into place easily while others are difficult and force us to make choices that can change the direction of our lives permanently. Although making choices seems difficult right now, having the right tool (the Bible) to guide us, and a bit of training, will help us make good choices that we will be proud of for years to come.

It is true that life can be very puzzling at times, but as

Christians we don't have to figure it out on our own. God has given us complete instructions to help us put each piece of our "life puzzle" together perfectly. The Bible gives us guidelines that apply to us today on any topic under the sun. Whether it's celebrating or grieving, choosing friends or dealing with our enemies, or just seeking God's guidance on any decision we need to make, His loving principles are all right there.

In this chapter, we will learn what Scripture teaches about peer pressure and how each of us can have the strength to resist this very powerful desire that we all have to "fit in." We will see what Scripture has to say about not giving in to our sinful desires and who our role model should be.

Yes, fitting in is important. But we don't have to compromise our beliefs or our relationship with the Lord to achieve the kind of friendships that will last a lifetime.

Read II Kings 17: 7-23

1. What external pressure was at the root of the Israelites' sins (vv. 8, 15b and 21b)?

2. What was the result of their persistent sinning (v. 23)?

3. Give an example of how we can be "enticed" by our peers into doing things that are sinful in God's eyes.

4. What are some things the world accepts as "normal" although God says they are wrong?

5. How can we know what is right and wrong? How do we know what to believe (Joshua 1: 8-9)?

Read Matthew 14: 1-12

6. Why did Herod promise to give Herodia's daughter, Salome, anything she wanted (v. 6)?

7. Does sin look pleasing to us sometimes? Give an example.

8. Did Herod feel good about giving Salome what she asked for (v. 9a)?

9. Why do you suppose Herod kept his promise (v. 9b)?

10. Do you make promises or say things when you are with your friends that you know are wrong, yet say them so your friends will like you? Give an example.

If we make promises which we know go against what we believe, like Herod, we may be too embarrassed to go back on our promise when all our friends are around. If we read God's Word regularly and ask God for wisdom, He will guide us through His Holy Spirit to do what is right. If our "friends" encourage us to do things that are clearly wrong, we need to evaluate whether these "friends" are truly friends.

Read Genesis 39: 1-22

11. What pressure does Joseph face when he is left in charge of his master's home (vv. 7 and 10a)?

12. What was Joseph's response (vv. 8 and 10b)?

13. Why do you think Joseph didn't even want to be near Potiphar's wife?

14. What can we learn from Joseph (II Timothy 2: 22)?

   God wants us to be leaders, not followers. We are to run the race to win the prize (I Cor. 9:24-25). If we are following the world, we cannot win the race God has set for us to run, because we are in the wrong race. We do not have to give in to what the world says is the "norm."
   God uses ordinary people like Joseph to make great leaders. If you continue reading the story of Joseph, you know that after he got out of prison, he was placed as second in command of Egypt (Gen. 41:41). God used him to save the lives of many people who would have starved to death in the seven year famine. We know that all of Joseph's success was due to his relationship with God. Throughout the story we read over and over again, "*and the Lord was with Joseph.*" The Lord is with us too.
   We can find encouragement in the fact that Jesus knows from personal experience how we feel. While Jesus was on earth, he suffered many temptations like the ones we face, yet He did not sin (Heb. 4:15).

Read Hebrews 2:18, 4:14-16

15. Who can help us when we are tempted (v. 2:18)? Why?

16. What instruction does Hebrews 4:16 give us?

Read I Corinthians 10:13

17. Are the temptations we face unique only to us? Why? Why not?

18. What does "*common to man*" mean?

19. What promise does God give us in this verse?

20. God promises to provide a "*way out*." What must we do when God provides the way out?

Our "life puzzle" will have many pieces which will require us to make tough choices. There will be temptations to do what our peers are doing. Understand that you are not alone. Each believer has the Holy Spirit to guide her along with God's Book of instructions. Let's make it our priority to study God's Word and meditate on it so that we may be able to know what God's will is for our lives.

Everyone experiences some degree of pressure to conform. Let us set ourselves apart to God and conform only to the likeness of Jesus Christ.

21. What can you do to prepare yourself for resisting the temptations that lie ahead? Will you pray and ask God to help you in this area?

"Do not conform any longer to the pattern of this world, but be transformed by the renewing of your mind. Then you will be able to test and approve what God's will is—his good, pleasing and perfect will."
Romans 12:2

Friendships

LESSON 7

"What a man desires is unfailing love" (Proverbs 19:22a).
Everyone has the need to be loved and accepted and to have close
relationships with others. Scripture gives us hundreds of verses on
the topic of friends and friendship. In the NIV version of the Bible,
the words *friend, friends* and *friendship* appear 169 times in 163
verses. In the Bible we see examples of godly friendships as well
as betrayals by so-called "friends." God made us to be relational.

It is clear that from birth human beings need to be loved. A
study involving 91 infants in a Foundling Home outside the United
States proved this theory to be true. In this institution, the children
were breast-fed by their mothers, or by one of the other mothers if
their mother was not available during their first three months of life.
At the end of this period, the children were tested and found to be
developing at a "normal" rate compared to average children living
in the same city.

After the third month the children were separated from their
mothers. The children remained in the Foundling Home where
they were adequately taken care of in every respect. They were
kept clean and received better food and medical care than children
in other institutions that were observed. The only difference was
that there was only one nurse to care for up to twelve infants,
therefore, the children were deprived of the love normally provided
by their mother. The results of the observation were incredible. At
the end of the study, all infants had deteriorated drastically. They
were physically smaller in size and

more susceptible to illness. Of the 91 infants, twenty-seven died in the first year, seven died in the second year, and the remaining infants were either placed in families, other institutions or remained at the Foundling Home.[1]

The same results are true to some extent for older children and adults. Those of us who enjoy close friendships tend to be happier, and therefore, healthier. Medical studies prove that people who are loners, either by choice or circumstances, tend to get sick more often, stay sick longer, and are generally less happy than those of us who enjoy close friendships.[2]

Friendships are important. From the time we are born, most of us are given love and acceptance from our parents, who are the only friends we need at this point. This love is very satisfying and there is little, if any, need to find others outside of our family to love and accept us. As we approach adolescence, however, we are more aware of others within our own age group and develop a natural desire to be loved and accepted by our peers. This desire to be loved and accepted is so great that, as we studied last week, we sometimes make big mistakes in order to satisfy our need.

Because friendships are so important to us, it is crucial that we learn how to determine what a good friend looks like. I can't tell you how many times my mother told me to be careful in choosing my friends or counseled me concerning certain friendships. She had this saying that would drive me nuts. "Tell me who your friends are, and I'll tell you who *you* are." I can honestly say that I didn't like being told by my mother who I should or shouldn't be friends with, but I can also tell you that, looking back, my mother was right. As a matter of fact, Proverbs 13:20 tells us *"He who walks with the wise grows wise, but a companion of fools suffers harm."* None of us likes being told who our friends should be. Therefore, if we know what qualities to look for in a good friend, we won't have to suffer the consequences that bad company brings.

Choosing friends requires wisdom and discernment. It is also important to know that some of our friendships will be deeper than others. There are different depths of friendships. In the first category there are our friends from school, church, and regular after-school activities. These are friends we see often, but we don't necessarily spend a lot of time alone with. These are considered "casual" friends and we may have many friends of this

47

type. Out of those friends, there will be some who are a bit more special to us, so we will invite them over occasionally and enjoy each other's company. These friends can be called "close" friends, because we may have some things in common with them. However, we may not feel comfortable telling them our deepest feelings, and therefore, they do not qualify for the "best" friends group. There can be several friends who will fall into the "close" friend category. Out of these "close" friends, there will usually be a friend or two with whom we have many things in common and can openly share what's on our heart. These special friends are the ones we prefer to spend time with and with whom we have the most fun. This classification is the "best" friend category and is the group of friends that we will spend time learning about. God gives us beautiful examples of extraordinary friendships that teach us what qualities our "best" friends should have and what it takes for us to be the godly friends we need to be.

Good friendships have many benefits. True friends give us encouragement, love, and acceptance. They are self-sacrificing and are *always* there when we need them. They listen to us when we have problems and give us godly advice. They love and accept us even when they know our deepest, darkest experiences, and they continually lead us back to God so that we can grow spiritually. They can be trusted to keep to themselves what we have told them. We can have confidence that they will not gossip about us. They stick up for us when others put us down and will stay with us to the end.

In this chapter we will explore why friendship is necessary. We will study some beautiful biblical examples of godly friendships and the qualities these friends possessed. God loves us and wants to protect us from the harm of walking with fools, so He gives us examples of some bad friendships also, and shows us what some wrong reasons for friendship are. We will explore what Scripture says about encouragement and loyalty. Jesus Himself gives us a pattern to follow in the amount and quality of time He spent with His friends. Finally, we will determine what our response should be when a friend lets us down, and how to *repay* the evil that has been done to us.

Read Ecclesiastes 4:9-12

1. According to these verses, why is friendship important? List the benefits.

2. What do you think the author of Ecclesiastes meant by "a cord of three strands is not easily broken" (v.12b)?

Read I Samuel 18: 1-4; 19:1-7; 20; 23:16-18

3. What kind of friendship did Jonathan have with David (vv.18:1 & 3)?

4. Even though Jonathan was King Saul's oldest son and had the right to someday become king, what does verse 18:4 say Jonathan did for his friend?

5. What does this example of friendship teach us about self-sacrifice? Does this go along with what we learned from Philippians 2:3-4?

6. What good quality do we see in Jonathan as David's friend in verse 19:1-7?

7. King Saul was very jealous of David and wrongfully wanted to kill him (v. 19:4). What was Jonathan willing to do for his friend David (v. 20:4)?

8. How did Jonathan feel when he learned of his father's true feelings toward David (v. 20:34)?

9. What quality does I Samuel 20:39 show us a godly friendship should have?

10. How did these friends feel when they realized they had to part company (v. 20:41)? What made the parting easier (v. 42)?

11. Why do you think that David and Jonathan's friendship was so special? What was the main ingredient in their friendship (v. 20:42)?

12. According to verse 23:16, why did Jonathan go to visit David in the desert?

Jonathan's friendship with David was truly extraordinary. His love for his friend went beyond most friendships we see today, yet God used Jonathan's faithfulness to show us what real friendship is all about. Jonathan loved David as himself. He protected David when he knew he was in danger. Jonathan did what was right even when it meant going against his own father, the king. Jonathan gave up (sacrificed) his right to the throne willingly, knowing that his friend David would be the next king. The things he and David talked about were kept confidential. How could he do all this? His friendship with David was not based on his own interests. His interest was based on the covenants or vows he made to the Lord with David. Can any of us be a "Jonathan" to our friends? Yes! But only when the Lord holds the friendship together and when our friend's interest is more important to us than our own can we really become "true" friends.

Read II Samuel 9:1-13

13. According to these verses, what did David do even though his best friend Jonathan had died? Also see I Sam. 20:14-17. Is this a quality we should also try to attain?

Read Ruth 1:1-17

14. Even though Ruth had every right to stay in Moab, her own country, Ruth chose to go with Naomi. What do verses 16 and 17 tell us about commitment?

15. What wisdom and advice on friendship can we gain from the following verses?
a. Psalm 1:1

b. Psalm 55:12-14

c. Proverbs 12:25

d. Proverbs 16:28

e. Proverbs 17:17

f. Proverbs 18:24

It is important to remember that the most significant aspect of Jonathan and David's friendship was the fact that God was at the center of their relationship. This does not mean, however, that all of our friends must be Christians. Jesus Himself balanced the time He spent with believers and non-believers.

From the time that Jesus called the disciples (Matt. 4:19), to the time of His crucifixion (Matt. 27:46), most of His time was spent teaching and preaching. The crowds of people (non-believers) that Jesus taught, healed, and fed, can be considered "casual" friends of Jesus. These were friends with whom He shared spiritual truths and the message of salvation. From these crowds, Jesus had contact with several people whom He spent more time with, yet the time spent was also limited. These were people who were drawn to Jesus for one reason or another, and most of them had a need (Matt. 4:23; 8:3, 5, 14, 28; 9:2, 18, 27 etc.). What these people shared in common with Jesus was the faith they had, however big or small. Because Jesus had more contact with these people, we can consider them "close" friends. Scripture shows us, however, that Jesus spent a large amount of time with His twelve disciples, whom He selected to be intimately associated with (Luke 6:13). Jesus devoted His time to teaching, praying, encouraging, and leading them to a deeper knowledge of who He was, and what the Father's plans were. The disciples were Jesus' "best" friends. We know that of the twelve disciples, Jesus selected Peter, James, and John to spend extra time with Him (Mark 5:37; 9:2; 14:33).

Just as good friendships have many benefits, bad friendships can be devastating.

Read Matthew 26:14-16

16. What did Judas plan to do to Jesus, his "friend"? Why (John 12:6)?

17. Sometimes, despite the time, love and effort we spend on our friends, they may let us down. What should our response be (Matt. 18:21-22)?

18. Read Proverbs 19:4 & 6. Are these good reasons for friendship? Why? Why not?

What truths can we learn from all of this? Perhaps the most significant idea to consider is that our friendships can have a powerful influence on *who we become*. It is very important that our "best" friends share the same moral values and beliefs that we do. We need to be able to pray with our friends and to encourage each other to grow spiritually.

19. What are some qualities you would like to see in your "best" friend?

20. Based on the truths we have learned, are you willing to develop these qualities for your "best" friend?

Qualities "Best" Friends Possess

♥ They have a relationship with Jesus. Ps. 119:63

♥ They love and accept each other. 1 John 4:7

♥ They are good listeners and give godly advice. James. 1:19

♥ They keep conversations confidential. Prov. 16:28

♥ They stick up for one another. Prov. 18:24

♥ They are loyal and are there when needed. Eccles. 4:10

♥ They are willing to sacrifice for each other. Luke 14:10-11

♥ They pray for each other. Job 16:20

♥ They protect each other. I Cor. 13:6-7

"And let us consider how we may spur one another on toward love and good deeds. Let us not give up meeting together, as some are in the habit of doing, but let us encourage one another— and all the more as you see the Day approaching."
Hebrews 10:24-25

---

[1] René A. Spitz, *The First Year of Life,* (International Universities Press, Inc. 1977) pg. 278-281
[2] Blair Justice, *Who Gets Sick: Thinking and Health*, (Peak Press, Houston, 1987)

My Changing Body

LESSON 8

Of all the changes that take place throughout our lives after birth, the transformations that take place within our bodies during adolescence may be the ones that we remember always. This may not be the case for everyone, but it is true for most of us. This stage in our lives involves the most physical changes at the fastest rate we will probably ever see. Think about it. From the period starting at birth through, let's say, about ten to twelve years of age, we live in a wonderland, unaware of the reality that's about to hit. Granted, for the first ten or so years of our lives, we notice ourselves getting taller and getting better at doing things; however, these changes cannot compare with what is about to take place. Suddenly, WHAM! The next thing you know, **PUBERTY** hits and the race starts. Puberty is an amazing time period of about two years when a child's body changes into an adult's body. Hormones begin racing to all parts of our bodies screaming "*it's time to get ready for adulthood!*" We don't feel like adults, but we don't feel like kids either; as a matter of fact, we're really confused. We might wonder more than once, "What is going on with me anyway?" After these short years which are full of transformation, we have the rest of our lives to be adults. Considering all the changes going on, do we have a reason to be confused? Of course! Believe me, if you are confused, you are not alone. God knows every change that is to take place. Remember, He created our inmost being and has planned each change that must occur. In addition to the changes going on in our bodies, there are also changes going on in our environment.

There is the change from elementary to middle school then high school. Just when we felt comfortable living up to what was expected of us at the elementary level, we are told of all the new expectations we must now live up to. There are assignments to be turned in, schedules to memorize, textbooks to keep track of, grades to maintain, and as if that is not enough, we are to accept responsibility and have a good attitude while we're at it. Oh, and by the way, chances are that our friends are going through the same changes as well. It's enough to drive anyone crazy.

Of course, we will not all go through these changes at the exact same time. Some of us will start sooner and others will start later. Here are some of the physical changes that we can expect to take place, if they haven't already.

Our pituitary gland, which is located in our brain, starts sending hormones to several parts of our body alerting each part of the changes that must begin to take place. Soon, our breasts begin to develop and our hips widen a bit making us look more like women. We can expect hair to begin to grow in our pubic area as well as under our arms. Our ovaries, (refer to diagram on page 59) which up to this point were asleep, begin to release an egg each month (about every 28 days) which can barely be seen with our naked eye; this is called ovulation. A few days before the egg is released from the ovary, the lining of the uterus begins to thicken with blood to prepare for the egg to nestle itself in this lining should it be fertilized. The egg takes about five days to travel through the Fallopian tube into the uterus. If this egg is not fertilized by a sperm, the thick lining of the uterus is not needed. Both the unfertilized egg and the thick lining of the uterus are shed out of our body through the vagina. This is the time during the month when we will need to wear a pad or sanitary napkin. This process is called menstruation, menstrual period, or just "period," and happens about fourteen days after ovulation. You can expect this menstrual cycle to occur approximately every twenty-eight days and to last three to five days, except during pregnancy, or after the age of about 50, when periods stop altogether. Getting your period for the first time does not need to be frightening. You may feel like something is wrong, but it's all part of the wonderful way God has made us. It is common to have irregular periods the first couple of years. This may be caused by irregularity in the release of hormones from our brain or ovaries.

Menstruation is the most significant change that we will

undergo during puberty. This change is beautifully orchestrated by God to enable us to become mothers when we get married, should this be part of His plan. Some people have said that menstruation is dirty or awful, but this is untrue. Nothing God has created is awful or dirty. Menstruation is a wonderful gift from God which exclusively allows us, as women, to prepare a special place for babies to grow before they are born. How wonderful it is to know that God so carefully planned each detail of our lives. It is just another way God says, "I love you!"

Another change we can expect is the gradual development of our facial features which will make us look older. Take a look at your school picture and compare it to just a year or so ago. The only change which most of us will not welcome is acne. All the other changes we experience are mostly hidden under our clothes, but acne is visible to others. Don't despair though; proper hygiene and treatment will help keep acne under control. If you feel your acne is out of control, you can talk to your parents about making an appointment to see a doctor who will have answers to your particular problem.

This topic of "My Changing Body" will be divided into two lessons. The first lesson will discuss the physical changes we will be facing, some of which, perhaps, we have already begun to experience. By knowing the truth of what to expect, we can eliminate the lies, old wives' tales, or myths, which the world has so craftily adopted as truth. The first part of the study will focus on questions pertaining to the physical changes that take place during puberty, and questions frequently asked by girls. The second lesson will deal with our emotions since they can dominate so much of our lives.

Finally, we will allow an "open" question and answer session during this lesson, which will allow us to answer any questions that may not have been addressed. If you feel that you would prefer to ask a question confidentially, your group leader may choose to provide blank cards on which to do this. No names will be on the cards to ensure confidentiality. Please remember that one of the main purposes of this Bible study is to provide support to one another. Everything shared by the group is to remain within this group alone, therefore, the cards should not be necessary.

Uterus Diagram

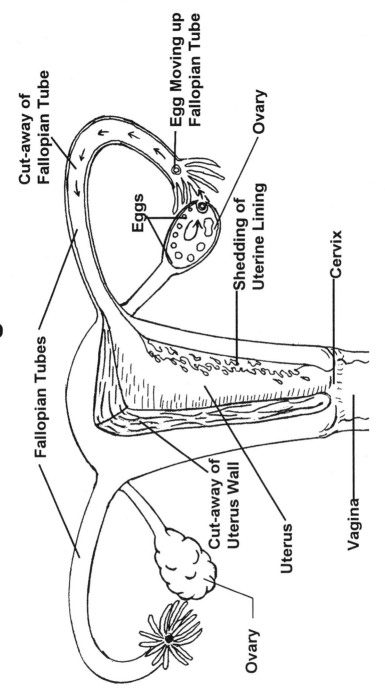

- Cut-away of Fallopian Tube
- Egg Moving up Fallopian Tube
- Ovary
- Eggs
- Shedding of Uterine Lining
- Cervix
- Fallopian Tubes
- Cut-away of Uterus Wall
- Uterus
- Vagina
- Ovary

"For you created my inmost being;
you knit me together in my mother's womb.
I praise you because I am fearfully and wonderfully made;
your works are wonderful,
I know that full well.
My frame was not hidden from you
when I was made in the secret place.
When I was woven together in the depths of the earth,
your eyes saw my unformed body.
All the days ordained for me
were written in your book
before one of them came to be."
Psalm 139: 13-16

1. Why do some girls get their period before other girls?

2. Are bigger breasts better than small ones? Why?

3. Can I use tampons? Will they hurt me?

4. Why do some people say that menstruation is a woman's curse?

5. Why do we sometimes get cramps and tenderness in our breasts before our period comes?

6. What is Pre-Menstrual Syndrome (PMS)?

7. What can I do to help ease symptoms like cramps or emotional ups and downs that come with my period?

8. Should I avoid exercise when I have my period?

9. Why does it sometimes hurt so much when your breasts grow? Does it ever stop hurting?

10. Does it hurt to have your period?

11. Considering the intricate detail which God lovingly used in forming our bodies, how should we feel about His concern for us?

12. God's love for us is so great that He is present with us even before we are born (Ps. 139: 16). How should this make us feel about God?

13. Write any questions you may have concerning the physical changes that take place during puberty.

"Every good and perfect gift is from above, coming down from the Father of the heavenly lights, who does not change like shifting shadows."
James 1:17

My Changing Body

LESSON 9

In addition to the physical changes we discussed in the previous lesson, the final change I would like to talk about, which we *all* experience, has to do with our emotions. During puberty and even for a few years afterwards, our emotions will go bonkers. It will often feel like we're on an emotional roller coaster. When we are excited, we will be even more excited and when we are disappointed, we will be devastated. When we like something, we will think we *love* it and when we dislike it, we will **hate** it. Our emotions are in an exaggerated mode during these years, and at this stage, we don't always have the needed experience to deal with them appropriately. *This is why it is so vital for us to learn to make decisions based on what we "know" rather than on what we "feel."* Believe it or not, our feelings have the tendency to deceive us. Jeremiah 17:9 states, " *The heart is deceitful above all things and beyond cure. Who can understand it?"* Adults experience this emotional dilemma as well. This does not mean our feelings will *always* lie to us, but more often than not, this tends to be true. During these years, it will be wise to run our "feelings" by our mom or a trusted, godly friend. The best way to know if we should go along with our "feelings" is to compare them to what God has to say in His Word. When we *know* what God teaches us through His Word, we can have confidence that we are making the right choices.

Emotions. What are they anyway? For the sake of this study, we will define emotions as strong feelings such as love, hate, loneliness, fear, guilt, depression, happiness, grief, and anger. Although we will not cover all of these emotions, it is good for us to be aware that they exist and are normal.

Read I Corinthians 13:4-8a

1. What role, if any, do these verses say emotions play in our demonstration of real love? Why?

2. According to these verses, is real love based on emotions or on commitment? Why?

3. God tells us in these verses that love is not self-seeking. What does this mean? What does the world around us say love is?

4. What is wrong with the world's view of love?

5. How long should real love last (v. 8a)? Was this the type of love we saw David express towards Jonathan and his family? What about Christ's love?

6. Knowing the truth of what real love looks like, are you willing to compare your "feelings" of love to the standards in I Corinthians 13:4-8a? Why?

Have you ever lain in bed at night and thought you heard a noise? I've had this experience many times, and I can tell you that it isn't fun. I have allowed my imagination to run wild, and as a result, I've been overwhelmed with fear that was unfounded. Let's take a look at the emotion of fear and how to overcome it.

Read Luke 12:4-7

7. Why are we not to fear men (v.4)?

8. Who is the only One we are to fear? Why (v.5)?

9. When we are afraid, where can we find comfort (Psalm 91)?

Read Ephesians 4:26

10. What does this verse tell us about anger? Is it OK to be angry? Why? Why not?

11. What must we do when we are angry? Why?

It is difficult to understand that our "feelings" are not accurate all the time. Although the Holy Spirit lives in us and will counsel and guide us, our feelings are not always all from God. How then do we know when to trust them? In his book, *Emotions: Can You Trust Them?*, Dr. James Dobson gives four steps we should use to test the validity of our "feelings" or impressions.[1] Here are four questions to ask yourself.

1. *Is it scriptural?* What does the Bible teach us about this situation? Read the Scripture in context, not just a verse or part of a verse.
2. *Is it right?* God's will always conforms to His biblical principles of morality and decency.
3. *Is it providential?* In other words, is it the right timing? Are the doors opening up for us, or are we trying to bust them open ourselves? If it is God's will, He will open the necessary doors for us and help things fall into place.
4. *Is it reasonable?* Does it make sense? Is it consistent with God's character to require it?

We must remember that some feelings will come from the desires we have deep inside. This doesn't mean they are not good; it just means we should act on what we know Scripture requires from us rather than on what society tells us is acceptable.

Remember to pray and ask God to guide you, and don't forget that waiting is an important part of making decisions. Another thing to keep in mind is that Scripture tells us that Satan himself masquerades (disguises himself) as an angel of light (II Cor. 11:14). Satan can trick us into believing that our feelings are from God if we are not alert.

After all this talk about change and confusion, you might be overwhelmed and wonder "Will the confusion related to adolescence ever end?" The answer is yes. As I said before, puberty lasts only about two years. By the time you reach about sixteen years of age, your hormones will be more balanced. There will still be more maturing to do, but the majority of drastic changes will have taken place.

In the midst of all the change, you can rest assured that God will never change (Numbers 23:19). God has made us just the way we are. We have every reason to feel good about who we are, and to enjoy the wonderful gifts we have received as women.

"Trust in the LORD with all your heart
and lean not on your own understanding;
in all your ways acknowledge him,
and he will make your paths straight.."
Proverbs 3:5-6

---

[1] James C. Dobson, *Emotions: Can You Trust Them?* (Ventura, CA: G/L Publications, 1980), pg. 134.

Boys And Sex

LESSON 10

After reading the title of this week's topic, you might ask yourself, "What could we possibly need to learn about boys?" It wasn't too long ago that you may have felt that boys were creatures who were strange, mean and "SICK," and as far as you were concerned, you stayed as far away from them as you could. Or perhaps you've reached the stage in your life where you might say, "Great, I want to know all I can!" Either way, what we will discuss in this lesson will help you become more informed about some differences between males and females, and help you make choices which will honor our heavenly Father, our parents, and ourselves.

God, through His Word, has revealed to us that He made males and females to complement each other. We know that through the creation of the world, God saw all that He had made and it was "*good.*" However, when it came to Adam, God said in Genesis 2:18, *"It is not good for the man to be alone. I will make a helper suitable for him."* What did God mean by that? 1) God began the practice of marriage. 2) God designed marriage; therefore, marriage is a spiritual act. The act of marriage brings a man and a woman together to be one in spiritual and physical unity for the purpose of serving God together as one. 3) Man was not complete without the woman. He was lonely even though God had given him dominion over all the creatures of the sea, sky and earth. 4) God made woman out of Adam's "side" (a rib). This reveals that man and woman were equally valuable to God and only when they are married do they complete each other. However, God clearly names the man as head of the family, just as Christ is the head of man, and God the head of Christ (I Cor.

11:3). 5) When man realized his solitude and loneliness, God made **one** special woman for Adam to be his partner for the rest of his life. 6) God declared that Eve was a "helper" for Adam. Since Scripture describes God as our helper also, this is a compliment and does not mean that Adam was superior to Eve.

What God said in those two short sentences in Genesis says so much, that we will have to limit this lesson to talking about the changes boys go through during puberty, sex and sexuality. In marriage, two people can find complete fulfillment as they enter the permanent relationship of husband and wife. However, not everybody chooses or has the opportunity to get married. This does not mean that they are incomplete or will not find true happiness.

We talked about girls and puberty, but what happens to boys while the girls are going through all these changes? Although boys will generally experience puberty later than girls, the changes are sure to come. This explains why it is not unusual for girls to be fascinated by boys while the boys couldn't care less about girls. During puberty, boys go through changes which take them from being little boys to becoming men. These changes in boys occur approximately between the ages of twelve to fourteen, but it is not uncommon for some boys to begin puberty later. As with girls, each boy is unique and will develop at his appointed time according to his genes.

As with girls, the pituitary gland sends messages to the necessary parts of a boy's body, telling them that it's time to wake up. A hormone called testosterone will circulate through the bloodstream and cause the growth of body hair, muscles, height and weight gain. The scrotum will increase in size and the testicles will begin to produce sperm, the penis will grow, and a voice change will occur. During this time boys will often feel awkward about the way they look and sound. These changes are as difficult for boys to go through as it is for girls to go through their changes. It is important to be kind to one another during this very confusing time. Good friends always encourage and cause one another to grow spiritually.

At the end of this transformation, the boy's body has become that of a man and he is capable of making a girl pregnant. As with girls, though, there is a lot of maturing that has to take place before he can actually take on the responsibility of protecting his wife and providing for a family. After puberty is over, the "construction" is nearly finished, but the "remodeling" has to continue so that we can grow in maturity, spirituality, and holiness. During this time it is very important that both young men and young women maintain proper relationships and know **the truth** about sex.

What does sex mean anyway? One definition of sex according to Webster's dictionary is the gender or "the character of being male or female; all the attributes by which males and females are distinguished." Another meaning of the word sex is sexual intercourse. God intended sexual intercourse or "sex" to be a wonderful part of marriage. It was His idea, not ours. God created sex as part of His plan for a man and his wife to enjoy. Therefore, sex is a holy act *in* marriage. Within marriage it is not dirty or wrong. When a man and a woman are married and have sexual intercourse, they become one flesh. Their bodies become one. This perfect closeness or unity that God intended only for married couples causes them to bond together. Before Eve was created, she was one with Adam as a part of his body. When God created her from Adam, they became two separate individuals. In marriage, the two individuals are again bonded together as "one flesh," yet, each person retains a unique personality. Sex is a gift from God that a woman gives to her husband and a man gives to his wife. Before men and women have sexual intercourse, they are said to be virgins; that is, they have never had sexual intercourse. When a man and woman get married, they each bring into the marriage a special gift that no one else on earth can give for them: it is the gift of their virginity or sexual purity. That means that they both saved that very special part of themselves for the **one** man or woman that God has called to be their husband or wife.

Unfortunately, most of the examples we see or hear in the world today don't go along with what God intended. As a result, there are many bad consequences that can occur if you should choose to go against what God has established as right. The world is filled with lies that can lead you to do things that you know are wrong. For example, we have all heard people say if you are really in "love" then it's OK to have sex. But, after studying the truth about our emotions, we know that love is a commitment, not a feeling or an emotion. Our feelings can *and will* trick us when we're in love. When you make a commitment to love someone, it will be very normal to have a desire to be very close with that special person or even think about having sexual intercourse. God made us sexual beings. Since we know that these feelings are normal, it is necessary that you decide now, **before you**

begin to date, to remain sexually pure until you are married. Some young people have decided to make a vow before God and their parents to abstain from having sexual intercourse until after they are married. When they make this vow, they receive a ring or a symbol from their parents to remind them of the promise they have made before the Lord. Aside from all this, if you really *love* someone, you will have the desire to respect them and uphold what God has ordained as sacred.

In this lesson we will discuss what God says about sex in His Word, the consequences that can occur if we go against what God has planned for us, and some biblical advice to help us live a life that will be richly blessed and bring honor and glory to our Lord. At the end of the session we will have an open question and answer time.

Read Genesis 1:27-31

1. According to verse 31, how did God feel after He evaluated His creation of man and woman?

2. At the end of each day of creation, God evaluated His work and gave it approval. Why do you suppose God was more pleased when He created man and woman?

Read Genesis 2:18-25

3. What do you think verse 24 means?

4. How do you feel when you're taking a shower or dressing and someone (such as your mother, brother, or friend) walks in and sees you naked? Why?

5. Why do you think Adam and Eve were naked and not ashamed?

In a marriage relationship, neither the husband nor wife has to feel used or exploited by the other partner; therefore, there is no need to fear or have shame. This was God's plan. On the contrary, when a man and woman have sexual intercourse outside of marriage, there is **no** vow, promise or commitment that holds the relationship together before God or society. Sex outside of marriage is not God's plan; it is man's sin. Premarital sex is destructive, hurtful, and will cause you to have guilt and shame. Psalm 19:13.

6. What are some consequences that can occur should you choose to have sex before marriage?

1)

2)

3)

4)

5)

7. What is "Safe Sex?" Is it really safe? Why?

8. When is a good time to decide to remain sexually pure until after marriage? Why?

·9. What is God's view about sex according to what we have read in the Bible?

Read I Corinthians 6:9-20

10. From these verses, we know that everything is permissible but not beneficial. What do verses 9 and 13 say about sexual immorality?

11. What is the body meant for (v. 13b)?

12. Because our bodies are the temple of the Lord, what wisdom can you learn from these verses?

13. Explain what verse 18 means in your own words.

14. Write verse 19 in your own words and share your meaning with the group.

15. How are we to honor God (v.20)?

Read I Thessalonians 4:3-7

16. How does God want us to control our bodies, and where can we find the strength to do it (Philippians 4:13)?

17. What are the advantages of waiting to have sex until after marriage?

18. What does Hebrews 13:4 say about marriage and sex?

There are cases in which a young girl has been the victim of rape, sexual abuse, or molestation. If this is true for you please understand that this offense was not your fault; *you were the victim*. There is no reason why you should feel that it is too late for you to make a promise of sexual purity before the Lord. As a matter of fact, there may be someone in this group who has been tricked into having sex or made the mistake of believing the lie that if you love someone, you should have sex. God accepts us right where we are no matter what has happened to us or what we have chosen for ourselves. It's never too late to turn to God for healing and/or forgiveness. God is *our* loving heavenly Father who will always love and receive us.

19. Knowing the truth we've discussed concerning sex and marriage, are you willing to make a vow before God and your parents to wait to have sex until after you are married?

20. Share any questions you may have which pertain to today's lesson.

"For this reason a man will leave his father and mother and be united to his wife, and they will become one flesh. The man and his wife were both naked, and they felt no shame."

Genesis 2:24-25

Healthy Relationships

LESSON 11

"*But for Adam, no suitable helper was found*" (Gen. 2:20). What is it about relationships that is so attractive and captivating? What are we really searching for when we look for that perfect person whom we will love and want to marry? According to Scripture, "*What a man desires is unfailing love*" (Prov. 19:22a). What does this mean? We are all made by God to have a special relationship (Gen. 2:18). The male-female relationship is one of the most important in all of God's creation aside from our relationship to God. But what are we looking for?

As we discussed in Lesson 7, we *all* need to be loved and accepted. From a very young age, we make plans for our future which almost always include being loved and honored by a very special someone who will always be faithful to us. Most of us have daydreamed about how great it is going to be to grow up, get married, and have someone of our very own who loves us unconditionally. This type of thinking is normal and good because what we are all looking for is unfailing love.

But, how do we *find* unfailing love? In Lesson 6, we talked about our "life puzzle." If you remember, in order for the pieces of our "life puzzle" to fit together properly, there is a certain order that must be followed. Unfortunately, even when we feel we have followed God's instructions, sometimes things don't always work out the way we planned. Why does this happen? There are many factors that can affect what we will call the "fairy tale" marriage, or healthy relationships. In today's lesson, we will focus on several elements that influence healthy relationships.

The first factor that can affect the fulfillment of our dream of finding unfailing love is that we often look for it in the wrong places. We must understand that unfailing love can *only* be found in God. As human beings, we are terribly imperfect and are powerless to offer unfailing love to anyone consistently. God, on the other hand, *is* perfect and *is* capable of loving us with a love that is unfailing, unconditional, and everlasting. If we do not have a solid relationship with God, we cannot experience the unfailing love we so desperately look for. Knowing that our need for unfailing love can be found only in God, we should make it a priority to have an intimate relationship with Him. This type of relationship begins when we accept Christ as our personal Savior, and believe that He is God and that He died on the cross and was resurrected so that our sins would no longer have power over us. As in any relationship, intimacy with God requires time and effort. This means we must read His Word every day and spend time talking to Him in prayer. When we spend quality time with God we begin to understand how much He loves us, how well He knows us, and how He will meet all our needs (Phil. 4:19).

Having a close relationship with God is the key to experiencing His unfailing love. However, just as it is important for each one of us to have a solid relationship with God, it is also crucial for our future mate to have one as well. It will be impossible for a man to know what unfailing love is if he himself has not benefited from it. How can a man understand how God wants him to love you if he does not know God? The Bible tells husbands that they are to love their wives just as Christ loves the church (Eph. 5:25). Christ gave His life up for the church. Husbands should be willing to do the same for their wives. This does not mean that a husband must die for his wife. This means that a husband must seek *the highest good* for his wife. A husband is called by God to love his wife just as much as he loves himself (Eph. 5: 28), and he is to put his wife before himself. Only when a husband knows God personally can he accomplish the important role he has been called to fill as husband.

In marriage, when a couple is committed to God, they are able to uphold their God-given responsibilities to each other. That is, a wife is to submit to her husband as to the Lord (Eph. 5:22) and a husband is to love his wife as Christ loved the church and gave Himself for her. These commands to both husbands and wives are intended to bring a beautiful balance of unselfish giving to each other. If a husband seeks the highest good for his wife, he will not consider her a "slave" in her submission to him. Also, if a husband loves his wife as himself, he would never harm or mistreat her, since it would be as if he were harming himself. God's plans are always perfect. They are never intended for the benefit of one person, but for the benefit of all. God loves us and has planned that all who love and obey Him will be blessed.

When we choose relationships in which both people love the Lord, there is much more probability that a "fairy tale" marriage can be achieved. Unfortunately, many people do not believe that following God's plan is necessary for true happiness, so they spend their lives looking for unfailing love in the arms of anyone who will say "I love you."

I have counseled many girls who were sure that their boyfriends "really" loved them, so they had sexual intercourse with them only to find out later that they had been used and rejected. Sometimes they were left pregnant and alone. These sad stories are far too common today.

There was an article in the Tucson newspaper titled "Sex, lies, no videotape: Boys speak candidly," [1] in which two "clean-cut" Tucson High boys were interviewed concerning their attitude towards sex. The words they said are not the words any parent or young woman would like to hear, but it is important for us all to be aware that these "nice-looking" boys are out there. Here are just a few things they said quoted directly from this article. Try to identify whose best interest is focused on in each of these quotes. How do each of these "tactics" work? I have highlighted some words which may give you a clue.

"Trying to get women is a competition. It turns into a **game**, and you **use** the same lines with every one of them."

"Or **you say** you don't believe in pre-marital sex unless **you** love the person. And then **they want to hear** you say that you love them, so you love them for 20 minutes. And when they say, 'Well, what's going to happen tomorrow at school?' You say 'Well let's just **play** it by ear.' And then when tomorrow comes, **you act** as if nothing happened."

"I know the girls **I can get**: the ones with low self-esteem and the ones you know if **you say**, 'I love you,' they'll melt. Some guys even cry, **just to make** girls feel for them. Or you listen if they have a problem, and they think you're real sensitive."

"The girls that you want for a girlfriend are the girls that will tell you, 'no.' "

"And the girls nobody talks about. That's real important." (Has a good reputation)

"And the kind you want to have sex with are virgins, because **you** don't want a disease."

It is hard to believe that these seemingly "nice" boys can use girls as objects in their "competitive game." If they were scruffy-looking drug users, at least you would know what to look out for, but as the reporter stated, these were nice looking, clean-cut boys. Even harder to believe is that the girls are falling for their lies and continue to allow themselves to be used, rejected, abandoned and hurt. Why does this type of behavior keep happening? It's simple. People need to be loved and refuse to accept God's way as the only way. Although it is far less frequent, this type of exploitation also happens to boys. There are girls who will trick boys into believing that they truly love them in order to get them to consent to have sex with them. If the boy refuses to give in, he is called all sorts of names and accused of being a homosexual.

I feel very fortunate to have grown up with two brothers who loved and protected me and a father who treated me like a princess. They would tell me "guy" stories which helped open my eyes to what some boys really want from girls. They would always warn me if they saw I was making friends with a boy who might be trouble. Also, because I was so close to my brothers, most of my friends were boys. As a result, I did not go through the "boy craze" because I'd been around boys all the time. Being friends with boys helped me see boys as friends rather than dates. You may wonder how you should get to know boys if you don't have brothers or are not close to them. Your church youth group is a good place to start. Your parents may arrange activities which promote male-female friendships and they may rotate the responsibility of chaperoning the events. One important element that all healthy relationships have in common is close friendship.

How can we have a healthy relationship without the heartache? When is a good time to begin dating? Is dating a good way to get to know someone better? What about courting? What should I look for in my future husband? These are the type of questions we will try to address in today's lesson. As always, we will allow time for any questions you may have.

Read II Corinthians 6:14 - 7:1.

1. "Do not be yoked together with unbelievers." What does this mean (v.14)? Why?

2. Can we find harmony in a relationship with a non-believer (v.15)? Why? List reasons.

3. How can spending too much time around the wrong kind of people affect us? How should that affect our attitude toward dating unsaved people (vv. 6:17 & 7:1)?

4. Does this mean we are not to be friends with non-Christians? Why? Why not?

5. What advice can you give a friend who is thinking of dating a young man who is not a believer?

Read II Samuel 22:31-37

6. According to verse 31, what does it take for God to shield you?

7. According to this passage of Scripture, what are the benefits we can claim as God's children?

Read I Corinthians 10:13

8. What does this verse tell us about temptation?

9. Since God tells us that He will provide a way out of temptation, what should our response be (2 Timothy 2:22)?

Read Ephesians 6:10-18

10. How can we be strong in the Lord according to these verses? List the resources that are available to us.

11. These resources are not given to us just for accepting Christ. What must *we* do to benefit from God's resources (v. 11)?

Read Proverbs 31:30 & I Peter 3:3-5

12. According to these passages, where should we look for beauty in other people? Does this apply only to women?

       There are many ways to get to know people of the opposite sex. Presently, one of the methods most commonly used is dating. Today, most people think of dating as a way of getting to know lots of people and having fun. However, dating is supposed to be a way of getting to know one special person whom you may someday marry. The reason for dating this special person is to get to know them better in different situations. By dating one special person, you will have a good idea of how you relate to one another and you will discover what things you have in common. Another method that is becoming popular again today among some people is courting. Courting means that a young man who is interested in a young woman must contact her parent or parents and ask to take her out. A meeting is set up for the parent to meet the young man. At the meeting, the father or mother explains to the young man that he must be spiritually and financially prepared to marry if he falls in love. If the young man is serious about a relationship with the young woman he will be granted the opportunity to court. Part of the courtship will include inviting the young man to family gatherings, events, and activities. In an article in *Focus on the Family*, dated November 1995, Jim Ryun writes that he and his wife believe that courtship has "physical, emotional and spiritual safeguards over dating." They believe dating encourages young people to think: "If I like my date, I will go out with him/her a few more times, however, if I don't like him/her, I can always break up." Ryun feels it doesn't make sense to train for a long-term relationship by engaging in several short term relationships.[2]

The question of when to begin dating or courting is going to depend entirely on what your parents feel is best for you and your family. I've heard many parents suggest that 16 is a good age to begin dating; however, some experts believe that dating should not begin until kids are in college. The reasoning behind this suggestion is that the young person will be more spiritually, emotionally, and intellectually mature to make the difficult choices which are part of healthy relationships.

Regardless of what approach your family chooses as the acceptable avenue for getting to know people of the opposite sex, it is important that both you and your parents begin praying right now, if they haven't already, for that special young man who will be your life-long companion if marriage is God's plan for you.

13. List the advantages and disadvantages of dating.
      Advantages   Disadvantages

14. List the advantages and disadvantages of courting.
      Advantages   Disadvantages

One way to be sure you don't get into a serious relationship with the wrong person is to decide before you start dating what particular godly qualities you would like to see in your husband. Then, make a rule for yourself not to date anyone who doesn't meet the godly requirements you have established and ask God to protect you in your decision. This way, you won't find yourself dating and falling in love with a person who doesn't have your standards or values.

15. On the page provided, list the godly qualities you would like to see in your future husband. Also list the characteristics you don't want him to have. Sign and date it and put it in a safe place so you can review it when you are ready to begin a healthy relationship.

Do not be yoked together with unbelievers. For what do righteousness and wickedness have in common? Or what fellowship can light have with darkness?
2 Corinthians 6:14

---

[1] Julie Szekely, *Sex, lies, no videotape: Boys speak candidly, Tucson Citizen,*(Tucson AZ, March 12, 1992).

[2] Jim and Anne Ryun, *Courtship Makes a Comeback; Focus on the Family with Dr. James Dobson,* (Colorado Springs CO, November 1995), pg. 10

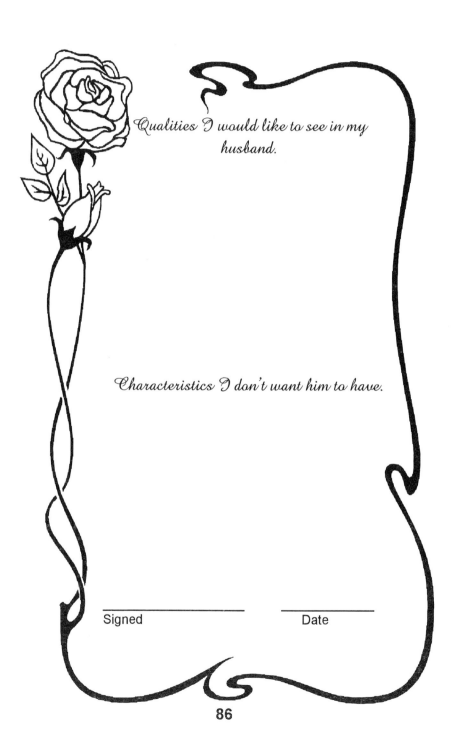

Qualities I would like to see in my husband.

Characteristics I don't want him to have.

_____   _____
Signed   Date

Can My Mom Understand?

LESSON 12

God has much to say about mothers. The NIV version of the Bible mentions mothers over two hundred and forty times. For most of us, our mothers are very important to us from the time we're born until we reach our early to mid-teens. There may be some of you whose mother was never a good role model or maybe you have never even met your mother. In any case, during puberty, our feelings towards our parents (or caregivers) sometimes change. Perhaps some of you can't imagine thinking that the high importance that you now have for your mother will ever change, while the rest of you are thinking; How did you know what I'm feeling? For some reason, when we reach this stage in our lives, our parents don't seem as awesome as they did when we were younger. We can all remember a time when we sincerely felt our mom and/or dad knew everything and could do anything. Somehow, on our way to adulthood, we lose the "super mom or dad" image of our parents and begin to allow dishonoring thoughts to replace the respect and value we once held for them. Some of us even go through a period when we feel our parents are not intelligent enough to understand what we are going through. The good news is that, miraculously, in our late teens even though the "super mom or dad" image is sometimes gone, our parents once again seem acceptable. Most of us will once again bond with our parents and the relationship will often be strengthened. What happens during our early teens? Do our parents go bonkers temporarily and then recover completely, or is there another side to this madness?

Thankfully, there is an explanation of why we sometimes feel our mothers can't possibly understand. As we discussed in Lesson 8, our bodies go through a remarkable metamorphosis in which we change from little girls to young women. During this transformation something that also changes is the way we see things. Things that once seemed innocent enough now take on a new dimension. For example, perhaps you know of someone whom you used to like quite well as a child, but you now think differently of that person. Perhaps this person is not as kind as you once thought, or possibly, he or she is not as honest as you believed.

As we get older we are able to see people from a different perspective which we were unaware of when we were children. This new insight involves discerning people's character, their values and beliefs, and evaluating whether their words match their actions. If we have high values and a solid belief in God, our perception of people is well-balanced since Christ is our model. However, if we take on worldly values and beliefs, our insight is distorted and inaccurate and we therefore tend to judge unfairly. As young children, we either like someone or we don't. As young women, we begin to understand **why** we like or dislike a person. This means we're able to see the imperfections in our parents' humanness and we may become quick to judge. We must remind ourselves that perfection is found only in Jesus Christ. Our parents are human and *will* make mistakes. None of us is perfect. We are all in the process of sanctification together; therefore, let us build one another up and encourage each other (Heb. 10:24-25).

During puberty, and for a while later, we are neither little girls nor quite yet young women. Therefore, we can't get a clear picture of what we are seeing in our parents or adults in general, so our usual response is to tune them out. Our attitude unfortunately is, "how can they possibly understand?" The sad part about this point of view is that this *is* precisely the time in our lives when we really need someone we can trust and turn to.

So, the question still remains. Can my mom understand? The answer is yes. If you are fortunate enough to have a mother or someone who has stepped forward as your mother to take this class with you, chances are they love you very much and are willing to dedicate time and effort to you and your future. Up to this point, we've spent over twelve weeks together, and God has been working on the hearts of both you and your mom. Also, don't forget that your mom has also been through infancy, childhood, puberty, and a good bit of adulthood, and as a result, has a lot of experience to draw from.

This lesson will take us through some passages of Scripture which will show us some special characteristics mothers possess. If we can see what mothers are willing to do for their children, it may help us understand what it's like to be a mother, and what God expects from us. We will also learn why God chooses older women to teach younger women and what role wisdom plays in this order. Finally, just for fun, we'll ask the moms some questions about growing up which may surprise all of us!

Read Exodus 1: 22 - 2:10

When Pharaoh's first orders were not adhered to by the Hebrew midwives, he ordered that a stricter policy be enforced. This time, he had his own people policing the Israelites.

1. What was Pharaoh's policy and how did this affect all the Israelite mothers?

2. What did Jochebed, Moses' mother, do to protect her baby?

3. Was Jochebed wrong to do this? What could happen if she got caught?

4. Why do you think she did it anyway?

Read I Kings 3:16-28

5. In your own words summarize what happened in this story.

6. Why did the real mother choose to give her baby to the other woman?

7. What do these two stories teach you about mothers?

Read Exodus 20:12

8. According to the fifth commandment, what will happen if we honor our father and mother?

9. What does honor mean?

Read Exodus 21:15 & 17

10. The home is so important to God that children are *expected* to treat their parents with the highest respect. What happened to the Israelite children who verbally abused their parents or mistreated them?

11. It's a good thing that the law doesn't allow us to kill kids who verbally abuse or mistreat their parents today. However, they don't just get away with it. What are some consequences that may occur in today's society if we dishonor our parents?

Read Titus 2:3-5

12. Make a list of what older women are called by God to do. What are they to teach younger women?

13. Why do you think God uses older women (Job 12:12)?

14. Make a list of the good qualities mothers possess.

15. As you consider the truth of what God commands us to do as children, what can you do to honor your parents even when you see their imperfections?

16. Realizing the extent that mothers will go to in protecting and taking care of their children, how should you behave toward your mom?

17. What can you do to maintain a good relationship with your mother?

Questions for Mom

1. What was the most embarrassing moment in your teen years?

2. Did a friend ever let you down? What happened, and how did you feel?

3. What was the craziest thing you ever did due to peer pressure?

4. Tell of a time you disobeyed and got caught. What did your mom or dad do?

5. Why do you think your daughter should trust you to understand her problems, and what can you do to help her gain confidence?

Godliness and holiness begin in the home. If parents cannot *model* a life that is consistent with their professed faith, children will neither honor and respect their parents or choose to follow God. Furthermore, our talk of God and our beliefs must match our walk with God in our actions so that our values, beliefs, and faith are valid for all who are watching.

"Dear children, let us not love with words or tongue but with actions and in truth. This then is how we know that we belong to the truth, and how we set our hearts at rest in his presence…"

I John 3:18-19

Temptations

LESSON 13

We have previously touched on the topic of temptation, yet we haven't explored it enough to understand why it is so powerful. Temptation is anything that entices us away from God and His ways. Temptation places us in a position where we question God's standards. Our areas of weakness, whether we are aware of them or not, provide an opportunity for temptation to seduce us if we rely on our own strength. However, because we cannot always easily recognize temptation in advance; we are often ensnared before we realize it. Just as the serpent convinced Eve that it was beneficial for her to eat the fruit, temptation gets us right in the heart and says; "God really didn't mean it that way, did He?" There are many reasons why we fall into temptation's snare, even when we are sincerely pursuing God's righteousness. The Bible gives us insight into how temptation works, what *we* can do to resist it, and who has the highest risk of giving in to it.

A good place to begin expanding our understanding of temptation's power is to examine how it works and where it comes from. Temptation is based on falsehood. It is directly related to lies and our willingness to compromise. Think of temptation as the deceitful force that is born from our own evil desires or from the devil himself. In the beginning, there was only truth. The force of temptation was successful after the serpent lied and gave Eve an opportunity to compromise on what she *knew* was true. The devil's "craftiness" overpowered Eve's innocence. If we don't have a good understanding of how the devil tries to mislead us, we too will be led astray. Bible commentators often classify temptation into three categories as seen in Eve's temptation in

Genesis 3:6; "*When the woman saw that the fruit of the tree was* **good for food** *and* **pleasing to the eye***, and also* **desirable for gaining** *wisdom, she took some and ate it. She also gave some to her husband, who was with her, and he ate it.*" These three categories which appeal to our inner being are: lust of the eye (pleasing to the eye), lust of the flesh (what feels good), and pride, glory, or status (popularity, recognition, self importance).

The first category of temptation, "lust of the eye," has such high success because it appeals to us as something very attractive. How could something that looks so good and seems so pleasing be so bad? Attraction is such a strong emotional force that if we don't use self-control, we become easy targets. As a matter of fact, it is so effective that advertisements often use the attraction "tool" to successfully tempt us into buying their "beautiful" new car or the latest fashion craze. Television ads make their products so appealing that lawmakers have had to step in and enforce guidelines to keep advertisers honest. Genesis 3:6 states that Eve saw that the fruit was "pleasing to the eye." If the forbidden fruit had been horrible looking, Eve may not have had any trouble turning away. Unfortunately, because the object of our temptation often looks so good, we will be lured into its trap if we don't have a solid knowledge of God's principles.

The temptations which fall under the category of "lust of the flesh" are often those which cause us to focus on our own pleasure. In other words, "if it feels good, do it." The world around us gives us the message that we should pursue *anything* that personally feels good regardless of what effect it may have on others, or on our relationship with God. We need to remember that God is not a mean killjoy who wants to take away all of our fun. Rather, He is a *loving father* who desires that our lives be filled with joy and happiness. The boundaries He has set for us are meant to protect us both physically and spiritually. God, in His wisdom, foresees the consequences that may occur when we overeat or diet unwisely, when we abuse alcohol or drugs, when we choose to become sexually active outside of marriage, or when we develop a slothful lifestyle. Remember, when Eve saw that the forbidden fruit was "good for food" she ate it (Gen. 3:6). Suddenly, all the other fruit God had provided for her was not enough. She now had to have *one more fruit*. Did God not provide adequately for Adam and Eve? Does Scripture not tell us that "*God will meet all your needs according to His riches in Christ Jesus*" (Phil. 4:19)?

Finally, the last category of temptation which we will

discuss is our inner desire for power, glory, or status. Why do you think most of us try out for the leading roles in plays? If I get the part, everyone will think I'm great. Wanting the leading role in a play is not a sin. As a matter of fact, God tells us in his Word that "*whatever you do, work at it with all your heart, as working for the Lord*" (Col. 3:23). Sin comes in when we do the hard work for our own glory. Scripture tells us that we are to let our light shine before men so that people may see our good deeds and praise our Father in heaven (Matt. 5:16). This means we are to give God the glory for **all** of our accomplishments. After all, God is the One who gives us the gifts we have, so it is fitting that we give Him the glory. Does this mean we, as Christians, are not to be in the spotlight of our community? In Paul's words, "By no means!" As Christians, we need to be out in the forefront showing the world what God's people look like, putting forth our highest effort with excellence and love, and giving Him the honor and glory. However, when we pursue fame, power, or glory for **our own** personal satisfaction and gain, we will be ensnared by temptation and sin. Eve saw that eating the forbidden fruit would give **her** God's wisdom, so she ate it and fell into Satan's trap.

Scripture tells us that God gives us wisdom, knowledge, and understanding if we seek it with all our heart (Prov. 2:3-6). We do not have to try to snatch it from God, like Eve did, because He wants us to have it. If temptation came with red flags, sirens, and bells we might be on guard and it would be easy to stay clear from it. However, because it is disguised as something we often desire or think we need, there is only one way for us to be victorious; by reading God's Word and asking God for the wisdom that only He can give.

Let's read some passages of Scripture together and see if we can find the three categories of temptation we've discussed hidden in the passage. In this passage it may be difficult to identify the categories of temptation, so let's stop and ask God for the wisdom to help us before we begin to read His Word.

Read Matthew 4:1-11

1. In verse 3, what category of temptation was Satan trying to trap Jesus with? Why did Satan think it might work (v. 2)?

2. What category would the temptation in verse 6 fall into? Why?

3. In verses 8 & 9, Satan again tries to ensnare Jesus. What category can you put this temptation into? Why?

4. Why was Jesus able to resist Satan and his lies (vv. 4, 7 & 10)?

5. What does this teach us about studying, meditating on, and memorizing Scripture? Why?

6. Does Jesus really know how we feel when we are tempted (Heb. 2:18)? Why?

Read James 1:12-18

7. What causes us to fall into temptation (v.14)?

8. What does giving in to our desires lead to (v.15)?

9. Where can we expect good gifts to come from (v.17)? Is there a price?

Read Proverbs 9:10-18

10. Who are the people who are at the greatest risk of giving in to temptation (v.16)? Why (v.18)?

11. How can we gain wisdom and understanding (v.10)?

Read Proverbs 2:1-11

12. What are the eight examples of efforts we can use to attain wisdom (v. 1-4)?

1.   2.   3.   4.

5.   6.   7.   8.

13. What are the benefits of putting forth this type of effort (vv. 6-11)?

1.   2.   3.   4.

5.   6.   7.   8.

Temptation has been around for a long time and it is not going to go away until we reach heaven. Satan is a master liar, and his promises never turn out the way he makes you think they will (John 8:44) . We must, therefore, be alert and *"Watch and pray so that you will not fall into temptation. The spirit is willing, but the body is weak"* (Mark 14:38). We must realize that when we consider compromising God's Word, we have taken the first step into Satan's trap.

14. Are you willing to commit to reading God's Word daily and to pray and ask for His wisdom?

How to Resist Temptation

✟ Read God's Word daily, and meditate on it (Joshua 1:8).

✟ Talk to God in prayer regularly and ask for wisdom, knowledge, and understanding (James 1:5).

✟ Hide God's word in your heart (Psalm 119:11).

✟ Put on the full armor of God (Ephesians 6:11).

✟ Have "zero tolerance" for compromising on what God has said (Joshua 1:7).

✟ Stay away from people who entice you to do what is wrong (Proverbs 1:10-17).

✟ Don't give in to your evil desires, yet pursue what is good (1 Timothy 6:11).

✟ If something causes you to sin, do away with it (Matthew 18:8-9).

✟ Be alert, watch, and pray (Mark 14:38).

✟ Know that God will provide a way out (1 Corinthians 10:13). Look for it.

"Consider Him who endured such opposition from sinful men, so that you will not grow weary and lose heart. In your struggle against sin, you have not yet resisted to the point of shedding your blood."

Hebrews 12:3-4

Purity

LESSON 14

When we hear the word "pure," some of us automatically think of crystal clear water, freshly fallen snow, or the color white. These are good mental pictures which are frequently used to symbolize purity. Perhaps you may think of sexual purity since we've discussed sexual abstinence before marriage as a form of purity. This too is a good thought since it is an important part of what is required for complete spiritual purity. For the purpose of today's lesson, let's define purity as the holiness or sanctification which takes place in the life of a believer as a result of faith in Christ and the indwelling of the Holy Spirit, together with the transformation which slowly takes place as we read, study, and meditate on God's Word and choose to live according to His plan.

The Old Testament presents purity as a ceremonial type of cleansing which was a necessary part of worshiping God. It had to do with washing your body and your hands before you worshiped God at certain important ceremonies (Ex. 40:30-32). There were all sorts of regulations and laws which had to be followed for the "purification" to be complete and acceptable. A big problem with this type of purification was that it focused on the outward condition of the worshiper and became *just* a ritual which would be witnessed by all who watched. All people could "purify" themselves outwardly by performing these rituals, yet the purification of their heart went unattended (Mark 7:6-7). We know that the people of Israel fell into sin over and over again which was evidence of their inward condition.

In the New Testament, Jesus teaches that this type of outward purification is not good enough. The purification that Christ requires is the purification that takes place inside our hearts, not outside our bodies (Mark 7:15). The Jewish spiritual leaders rejected Christ's teaching because it meant that the traditions which they had followed for hundreds of years fell short of what was needed to be "clean" before God. Jesus' teachings say that real purification springs forth from the condition of our hearts and requires *complete* devotion to God through faith in Christ. A spiritually pure life does *not* come automatically; it comes from daily obedience to God and His Word.

You might be thinking, "there's no way I could possibly measure up to such purity." In a sense, you're right. There is no way *any* of us could possibly attain the level of purity God wants to see in us, on our own. That is *specifically* why Christ came to our rescue. God demonstrated His love for us by sending His only Son to die for our sins while we were still sinners (Rom. 5:8). Christ's death on the cross for all our impurities (sins) makes it possible for us to be declared 100 % pure (Heb. 13:12). When we repent of our sins and accept Jesus Christ as our Savior, our purity is such that the Holy Spirit comes and makes His home in us. We are now set apart for God and equipped for worshiping and serving Him. This part of purity (the complete cleansing of sin) is a gift; it is a fact (Heb. 10:10 &14). However, God's love for us was demonstrated to us in action: He sent His Son to die for us. Likewise, we are strongly advised to grow in purity (Heb.12:14). Our love for God requires action which must reflect the love we have for Him. Faith without action will not lead to purity (James 2:20). Purity is achieved when we submit our faith, feelings, thoughts, and actions to God (Mark 12:30).

Our feelings and thoughts reflect the condition of our heart. God has given us the ability to keep our feelings and thoughts private from those around us, yet not entirely. Have you ever been surprised when someone who knows you well can tell what you are thinking? God's Word tells us that these feelings and thoughts come out of us in the form of words or actions (Prov. 27:19). By our words or actions, others can see what's in our hearts. We are successful in hiding our feelings and thoughts from others to a certain degree, but God knows what we feel and think all the time. For us to achieve the purity that God wants us to have, we must read God's Word, which purifies (John17:17), and pray that the Holy Spirit who is at work in us will guard our feelings and thought life (Phil. 4:6-7).

Unlike our feelings and thoughts, our actions are seen by

all who are around us. This "peer pressure" influences us to behave appropriately to some extent. This is especially true when we are around people who are likely to hold us accountable. These people may include our parents, siblings, teachers, Christian friends, or activity sponsors. When we control our actions because others are holding us accountable, our motives are not entirely pure. It is good to have mutual accountability with others; however, purity is accomplished when our actions are driven by *our* desire to please God.

Some might think that pursuing purity will lead to a boring life. Don't be fooled by this misconception. Purity is freeing, whereas impurity brings with it the weight of shame, guilt, and consequences which eventually rob us of the genuine peace and joy available by living righteously. The world makes sin seem attractive, but we know that attraction is one of temptation's main characteristics. Having fun the world's way means separation from God. Longing for God and His righteousness produces a joy that will not fade away.

Read Matthew 5:1-12

1. In these twelve verses of Scripture, Jesus uses the word "blessed" nine times. What does it mean?

2. Why is being poor in spirit a blessing (v. 3)?

3. What does Jesus mean by "*blessed are those who mourn*" (v. 4)?

4. What characteristics does a "meek" person have (v. 5)?

5. What does verse 8 mean in your own words?

6. What do the qualities stated in verses 3-11 have in common?

7. Why is Jesus so concerned with our inward condition?

Read Philippians 4:5-9

8. Give two reasons why it's important to let our gentleness be evident to all?

9. What six items does Paul mention as proper thought patterns? What do they mean?

1.   2.   3.

4.   5.   6.

10. Why do you think God wants us to control our thoughts?

Read Matthew 15:10, 17-20

11. What can happen if we allow unwholesome thoughts to dominate our hearts and minds (v. 19)?

12. What does this tell us about the things we choose to listen to on the radio or watch on TV?

13. Purity is the result of sanctification. What do the following verses tell us about how or where purity can be found?
a. Acts 26:17-18

b. John 17:17

c. Ephesians 5:25-27

d. Romans 15:15-16

e. 1 Corinthians 1:2

f. 1 Thessalonians 5:23

      The physical transformation that takes place during our adolescence takes only a few years, but the spiritual one which takes place when we give our life to God takes an entire lifetime. As believers, the ongoing process of sanctification is not complete until we reach heaven. This inward transformation which slowly takes place in us results in purity. The evidence is seen in an outward life of holiness and godliness.

      The important thing to understand is that holiness is *demonstrated* on the outside by physical acts, but those physical acts *do not* make us holy. The outward physical acts are an overflow of the holiness which is taking place in our hearts. Since our sanctification is not yet complete, we should work to correct our mistakes or impurities, but we shouldn't be paralyzed by the guilt brought on by acknowledging that we are imperfect beings.

14. We are told to make every effort to live a life of holiness (Heb. 12:14). How should knowing this truth affect the way we feel, think, and act?

15. What can you begin doing today to help you grow in holiness?

"…he who began a good work in you will carry it on to completion until the day of Jesus Christ."
Philippians 1:6b

God's Mercy

LESSON 15

This study has helped us learn the truths of who God is, why He came to earth, what He wants from us, who we are in Christ, and what our response to Him should be. We have had the opportunity to commit our lives to God if we had never done so, or recommit our lives to Him based on the truths *we now know*. We have been given the freedom to commit our sexuality to the Lord by making a vow to Him to remain sexually pure before marriage. Through this study we have strengthened our relationship with God, with our mother or daughter, and with other members of the group. In spite of all this, if it were not for God's great mercy toward us, we would still be desperately lost. Today's lesson will help us understand what God's mercy is, how He demonstrates it to us, and what our response should be. As a result, we will understand the peace that is available to us when we experience God's mercy.

Mercy can be defined as the lovingkindness, affection, and loyalty expressed by God to us. God's mercy is the love and compassion He showers on those who are helpless and who need relief from their distress. Mercy is not based on what *we* do; therefore, it cannot be earned. It is the gracious undeserved service of the Superior (God) to the inferior (us). It is God's treatment of us as forgiven. Mercy is part of God's character (II Cor. 1:3).

God's mercy toward mankind is seen consistently throughout Scripture. As we followed God throughout the Old Testament, we saw His mercy first toward Adam and Eve when He provided garments of skins for them after they had sinned against Him. This lovingkindness displayed by God was freely

109

demonstrated to Adam and Eve as a result of His love for them, and not according to what they had done. For we know that they had done nothing to deserve the mercy of God. On the contrary, they had disobeyed God. Then we saw God's persistent display of mercy *poured out* to the Israelites repeatedly, despite their unending submission to idolatry and sin. Finally, in the New Testament we see God's unsurpassable mercy toward us in the sending of His Son. There is no way *any* of us could have earned the mercy God has shown us by providing a *total payment* for all our sins. After it was clear that we were powerlessly lost in utter sin, God's love and mercy were so great that He took our sins **as His own** (through Christ) and provided *full* payment for offenses He never committed. Scripture tells us that the payment for sin is death (Rom. 6:23). Since we all have sinned (Rom. 3:23), we all deserve to die (go to hell). Because God's desire is to have fellowship with us, if we receive what we deserve (hell), fellowship with God would be impossible for we know that nothing that is wicked (sinful) can come in contact with a holy God (Hab. 1:13a). Therefore, it is only because of God's mercy to us that we are freed from our bondage to sin. We sin; God pays. We live; Christ died (as payment for our sins). God's mercy is the ultimate display of undeserved lovingkindness, affection, and faithfulness to us.

The benefits of God's mercy are not *given* to all. However, they are *available* to all. Before anyone can partake of God's mercy, she *must* repent of her sins and ask for the gift of salvation. Only those who have been saved through God's grace (faith in Christ) can experience His mercy. Scripture tells us that *we* are to approach God so that we may receive mercy (Heb. 4:16). Considering God's gift of salvation together with His everlasting mercy, what should we as Christians do? Because God's mercy is demonstrated to us in *action,* we too should show God our love and commitment in our *actions*. Romans 12:1 tells us that when we take into account the mercy God has poured out on us, we should willingly give ourselves totally to God. This means our lives, as well as the activities we are involved in on a daily basis. Whether we are at school or at home, at work or at play, at church or in our community, our activities should bring honor to God. As mentioned before, our activities and thoughts are an expression of what is in our hearts.

Once we give our lives to God, His mercies to us never

end (Ps.136). Since God's mercy overflows to us, He wants us to show mercy to one another (James 2:13). God's mercy is demonstrated to us in many ways. One way God shows us His mercy is through His forgiveness; in turn, we must forgive others. Our forgiveness of others *must* be based on the fact that we have been forgiven and not on whether or not the person deserves to be forgiven. None of us deserves to be forgiven by God, yet we are. Mercy can also be shown to others by helping those in distress, showing compassion to those in need, and by keeping peace within the body of Christ (Col. 3:15). Scripture tells us we are to be merciful just as our Father in heaven is merciful (Luke 6:36). This means that God's character is to be exhibited in us, His people. Jesus said that when we treat each other with lovingkindness, we are blessed (Matt. 5:7).

So, what happens when we accept Christ, offer our lives and activities to God, try really hard to love and honor Him and do what is right, but make a mistake and sin?   We know that as a result of God's mercy, we have died to sin (Rom. 6 :2). Just as our faith in Christ "sets us apart for God" and gives us eternal life, our identification with Christ in His death, burial, and resurrection "separates us from sin," so that the power of sin (death) no longer has control over us. This means we are "set free" from sin (because Christ paid the price with His life), but sin itself is not dead; it still exists.   Scripture clearly tells us that if we claim to be without sin we deceive ourselves (1 John 1: 8). We *all* fall short of the glory of God (Rom. 3:23). That's why no matter how hard we try, we will sometimes fail. Scripture strongly advises us to live a life of holiness (Heb. 12:14), and as we learned in Lesson 14, we are to do it with all our hearts. However, because sin still exists, we will fall short and sin, since we are imperfect beings. One of the greatest benefits we receive from God's mercy is the peace we have in knowing that there is nothing that can separate us from the love of God, even when we sin (Rom. 8:39).

Read Psalm 103

1. David begins and ends this psalm with praise for God. Why did he have reason to praise God with all his heart (inmost being) (vv. 1-2)?

2. What mercies does David list as his reason for praising God (vv. 3-5)?

3. What does "*redeems my life from the pit*" mean? Has God done the same for us?

4. What is the meaning of verse 6 in your own words?

5. What characteristics does God's mercy have (vv. 8-12)?

6. On whom does God have mercy (v.13)?

7. How long does God's love for us last (v. 17)?

8. When we fear God, who else benefits (vv.17-18)?

Read Romans 12:1-2

9. To "urge" someone is to push them to take immediate action. Why does Paul "urge" believers to offer our bodies as "living sacrifices" to God (v. 1)?

10. What does "*offer your bodies as living sacrifices*" mean?

11. How is our sacrifice viewed (v. 1)?
    1)

    2)

    3)

12. As a result of our offering, what are we **not** to do (v. 2)? Why?

13. What does verse 2 tell us **we should** do?

14. As we mentioned before, the word "transform" means to be changed completely from one thing to another (little girls to women); what does it mean in this passage of Scripture?

15. What does verse 2 say must happen to our minds?

Read Romans 8: 31-39

16. Since it is God, by His mercy, who justifies us completely through faith in Christ, who or what can separate us from His love?

17. Since Satan is alive and well, we will all struggle with temptation and sin. What peace can you find in knowing the truth about the security of your salvation (vv. 37-39)?

18. How should this cause us to behave toward others (James 2:12-13)?

It is amazing to understand that there is nothing in the world that can take away our salvation. Of course, knowing this makes it easy to see why Satan tries so hard to make us stumble and fall. He knows that God will defend His princesses, but in the meantime Satan can cause us to feel extreme pain and guilt. Satan wants us to think that since we are awful (we all sin), there is no way God can accept us. We also know that Satan is a master liar. Many people in the world cannot see themselves as forgiven because their sin is so great in their own eyes. God tells us in his Word that *If we confess our sins, He is faithful and just and will forgive us our sins and purify us from all unrighteousness."* (I John 1:9). We are daughters of the King; crowned with His love and compassion (Ps. 103:4). There is no sin that God in His immense mercy cannot forgive.

19. Are you willing to go out and share these truths with helpless, hurting people?

Because of the LORD's great love we are not consumed,
for his compassions never fail.
They are new every morning;
great is your faithfulness.
Lamentations 3: 22-23